ERIC VOEGELIN'S PLATONIC
THEOLOGY

Philosophy of Consciousness and
Symbolization in a New Perspective

Ronald D. Srigley

The Edwin Mellen Press
Lewiston/Queenston/Lampeter

Library of Congress Cataloging-in-Publication Data

This volume has been registered with The Library of Congress.

ISBN 0-7734-9626-2

A CIP catalog record for this book
is available from the British Library.

The Edwin Mellen Press   The Edwin Mellen Press
Box 450   Box 67
Lewiston, New York   Queenston, Ontario
USA 14092   CANADA L0S 1L0

The Edwin Mellen Press, Ltd.
Lampeter, Dyfed, Wales
UNITED KINGDOM SA48 7DY

Printed in the United States of America

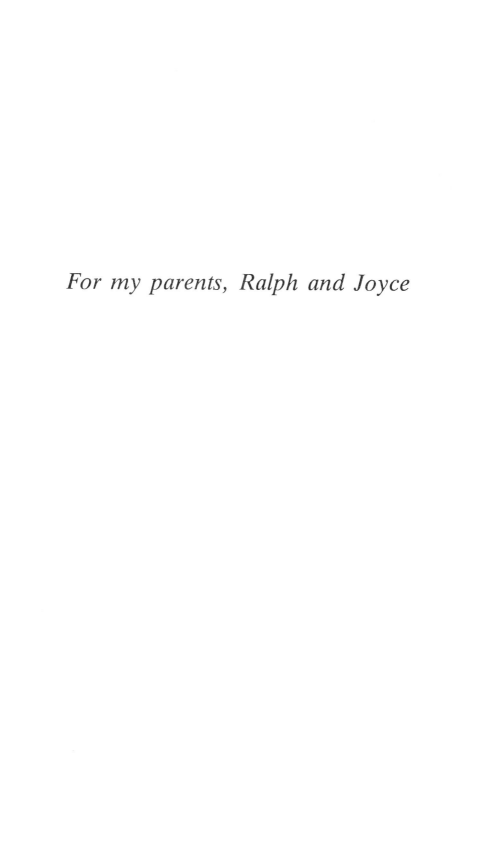

For my parents, Ralph and Joyce

TABLE OF CONTENTS

ABBREVIATIONS

Anamnesis	*Anamnesis*. G. Niemeyer, trans. & ed. (Notre Dame: University of Notre Dame Press, 1978).
AR	*Autobiographical Reflections*. E. Sandoz, ed. (Baton Rouge: Louisiana State University Press, 1989).
Conversations	*Conversations with Eric Voegelin*. E. O'Connor, ed. (Montreal: Thomas More Institute, 1980).
EESH	"Equivalences of Experience and Symbolization in History." *In Philosophical Studies*, XXVIII (1981), 88-107.
ER	*From Enlightenment to Revolution*. J. H. Hallowell, ed. (Durham: University Press, 1975).
IR	"Industrial Society in Search of Reason," *Technology and Human Destiny* (Michigan: University of Michigan Press, 1963).
OH I	*Order and History* Vol. I: *Israel and Revelation* (Baton Rouge: Louisiana State University Press, 1956).
OH II	*Order and History* Vol. II: *The World of the Polis* (Baton Rouge: Louisiana State University Press, 1957).
OH III	*Order and History* Vol. III: *Plato and Aristotle* (Baton Rouge: Louisiana State University Press, 1957).
OH IV	*Order and History* Vol. IV: *The Ecumenic Age* (Baton Rouge: Louisiana State University Press, 1974).
OH V	*Order and History* Vol. V: *In Search of Order* (Baton Rouge: Louisiana State University Press, 1987).

PREFACE

The history of Western philosophy has been characterized by an ongoing discussion about the relationship between theology and philosophy. This book is an attempt to understand the nature of this relationship through an analysis of Eric Voegelin's philosophy of consciousness and symbolization. I attempt to show how Voegelin's philosophical analysis of consciousness affords us insight into the nature of both true and false theology. My argument is based on Voegelin's discussion of the conception of theology developed by Plato in Book II of the *Republic*. According to Plato, the term "theology" is descriptive both of the symbolism of divine reality employed by consciousness and the state of consciousness that symbolism expresses. I argue, therefore, that an understanding of the various human responses to divine reality cannot be separated from an understanding of the true nature of consciousness and its deformation.

In the first chapter of this study I outline Voegelin's understanding of the true nature of consciousness and its symbolic expression. In Chapter Two I critically assess several deformative understandings of consciousness by placing them alongside Voegelin's analysis. My study concludes with a discussion of two questions that arise in response to the analysis of Chapters One and Two: (1) How is one to move from a state of deformation to a true state of existence? and (2) How is this true state established as true?

The task of this book, as I have outlined it above, is certainly not an easy one. And I am only too aware of the shortcomings of the analysis I offer in response to that task. Often times answers are offered too quickly and difficult questions are given only cursory treatment. Nonetheless it is my hope that the questions that are raised in these pages are important ones, and that the answers offered, inadequate as they may be, will serve to encourage further dialogue. If this much is achieved I will consider the work a success.

ACKNOWLEDGEMENTS

There are two people in particular to whom I am indebted for their thoughtful criticisms and suggestions regarding this manuscript. I would like to thank, first of all, Dr. Zdravko Planinc, without whose guidance and insight this work would likely never have been completed. Whatever real insight is apparent in this text has been decisively influenced by him. I would also like to thank Dr. Travis Kroeker, who has been a constant source of encouragement, and whose careful reading of the text saved me from many blunders.

I would also like to express my appreciation to Dr. Gérard Vallée for reading an earlier draft of this manuscript and to my friend and colleague Michael Root for his insightful comments and helpful suggestions. Thanks also go to Rita Ruffo for patiently preparing the final copy of the text.

I reserve special thanks for my parents, whose understanding and untiring support made the completion of this project possible.

This book is a study of Eric Voegelin's philosophy of consciousness and symbolization. More particularly, it is a study of his account of the experience and linguistic expression of divine reality. The book attempts to bring into relief the full import of Voegelin's analysis by juxtaposing it to several competing theories of consciousness prevalent in modern philosophical discourse.

The pertinence of Voegelin's philosophy for an analysis of questions concerning the divine or transcendent dimension of reality--questions which, in our time, are normally thought to be the concern of theologians or "religious thinkers"--is not likely to be fully evident to the reader. This lack of obvious pertinence is understandable, for in contemporary academic circles, philosophy, along with having painted itself into a corner with regard to even the most mundane philosophical questions, has well-nigh eliminated the question of God. [1]

---

[1] Concerning this handling of philosophical questions, consider Wittgenstein's remarks from *Culture and Value*: "People say again and again that philosophy doesn't really progress, that we are still occupied with the same philosophical problems as were the Greeks. But the people who say this don't understand why it has to be so. It is because our language has remained the same and keeps seducing us into asking the same questions. As long as there continues to be a verb 'to be' that looks as if it functions in the same way as 'to eat' and 'to drink', as long as we still have the adjectives 'identical', 'true', 'false', 'possible', as long as we continue to talk of a river of time, of an expanse of space, etc. etc., people will keep stumbling over the same puzzling difficulties and find themselves staring at something which no explanation seems capable of clearing up. And what's more, this satisfies a longing for the transcendent, because in so far as people think they can see the 'limits of human understanding,' they also believe of course that they can see beyond these." Ludwig Wittgenstein, *Culture and Value*, P. Winch, trans. (Chicago: The University of Chicago Press, 1980), 15e.

In a letter to his friend Alfred Schutz, Voegelin says that the "philosophical problems of transcendence are the decisive problems of philosophy" (*OH* V, 5). This remark is enough to point up the difference between Voegelin's understanding of philosophy and the version of it prevalent in modernity, yet it does not bring into analytic clarity the nature of the relationship between a philosophy of consciousness and the question of God, that is, the relationship between philosophy and theology. Here we must consult, as does Voegelin, the work of another philosopher--namely, Plato. Our return to Plato is not merely the consequence of an idiosyncratic preference on Voegelin's part--a bias toward classical philosophical texts--but is necessitated by the terms with which our inquiry is concerned.

Our first task is essentially etymological: given that words do not just appear out of nowhere but are created on a particular occasion by a particular person in order to express a certain type of experience of reality, we must, if we are to understand alright the relationship between "philosophy" and "theology", inquire where the terms originated. This leads us back to Plato, for "Plato created a neologism of world-historic consequences" when he coined the term *theologia* in Book II of the *Republic* (*QDD*, 579). The fact, then, that this ostensibly religious symbol was coined by a philosopher should be enough to assuage any initial fears concerning the legitimacy of our present endeavour.

The context in which Plato introduces the term *theologia* is a discussion of the difference between true (*alethos*) and false (*pseudos*) symbolic representations of the gods. This pair of terms has, as Voegelin asserts, "a long history." In the work of Hesiod, for example, there occurs the opposition of "his true history of the gods to current false stories" (*OH* III, 67). With Xenophanes, the distinction achieves even greater clarity through his introduction of the notion of "seemliness" (*epiprepei*). The older forms of symbolization--those employed by the poets--are unseemly, for they wrongly represent the gods, not simply by conceiving them anthropomorphically, but by attributing to them characteristics unsuitable even to mortal man: "Homer and Hesiod have ascribed to the gods all things that are a shame and disgrace among men, such as stealing, adultery, and cheating each other" (*OH* II, 172). In opposition to this conception, Xenophanes indicates that the "one God is greatest among gods and men, not like mortals in body or in thought" (*OH* II, 172). As Voegelin asserts, it is a "living being (*zoon*), though not of articulated form" (Ibid.). Concerning this God, however, Xenophanes was reluctant to claim certainty of knowledge: "There never was nor will be a man who knows about the gods and all the things I speak of. Even if by chance he should say the full truth, yet he would not know that he does so; there is fancy in all things" (Ibid.).

Xenophanes' notion of "seemliness" is a precursor of Plato's terms *aletheia* and *pseudos*. However, the meaning of Plato's terms is based on his newly differentiated understanding of divine reality as beyond being itself. God is no longer understood as a being who exists, albeit more eminently, alongside other things within the cosmos, but rather as the non-spatial, non-temporal divine ground of all that exists. And man, although incapable of cognitively comprehending this divine reality, is nonetheless aware of it through the erotic movement of consciousness toward the ground beyond the immanent order of things. According to Plato, then, *all* forms of symbolization, anthropomorphic or otherwise, that fall short of the new insight are understood as *pseudos*, as improper speech concerning the gods, while those that recognize the insight are *alethos*, proper speech.

In order to articulate this new insight, Plato coined the phrase *typoi peri theologias*, "types of theology." The phrase is intended to be descriptive of all forms of speech concerning the divine, including the radical denial of divine reality. This inclusiveness derives from Plato's awareness that the denial of God's existence, as much as its affirmation, is a response to the divine and, as such, constitutes a type of theology. The atheist, as much as the believer, speaks theologically, for he too symbolizes his experience of the divine, even if it is the experience of its absence. Plato, however, does not conduct his analysis solely on the level of symbolization, for theology is not merely a matter of words or speech, but of existence. He does not consider the examination of linguistic forms to alone provide a sufficient account. Language does not stand on its own but is an expression of one's state of existence, an expression of the nature of one's soul. Stated simply, well-ordered souls will express themselves in proper speech concerning the gods, while souls characterized by states of blindness, ignorance, and self-deception will engender improper forms of speech--forms of speech which reflect these deformative states. As Plato states concerning the negative pole of this dyad, "The falsehood in *words* is a copy of the affection in the soul, an afterrising image of it and not an altogether unmixed falsehood."[2] Regarding this "affection in the soul," Voegelin, citing Plato, states that "'to be deceived or uninformed in the soul about true being [*peri ta onta*]' means that 'the lie itself' [*hos alethos pseudos*] has taken possession of 'the highest part of himself' and steeped it into 'ignorance of the soul'" (*OH* III, 67-8).

In light of these remarks theology reveals itself, not simply as a matter of speech concerning the divine, but also as the states of consciousness that speech expresses. And here we find the basis for the resolution of our initial question, the question of the relationship between Voegelin's philosophy of consciousness and the symbolization of divine reality. The meaning of theological language is not autonomous, but contingent on the forms of consciousness that engender it. An analysis of theological types, therefore, must be carried out, not only on the level of language or speech, but also on the level of consciousness. Moreover, given the relationship of dependence between consciousness and symbolization, it may even be stated that proper speech about divine reality, that is, true theological language, "has no truth of its own." Voegelin asserts that the truth of Plato's "positive" theological propositions "is neither self-evident, nor a matter of logical proof; they would be just as empty as the negative ones, if they were not backed by the reality of the divine-human movement and counter-movement" (*QDD*, 580). A true theology is the linguistic manifestation of a well-ordered soul, of a consciousness ordered by its existence in truth, while a false theology is the symbolic representation of an "essential falsehood" in the soul, a *nosos*, or disease of the psyche.

---

[2]Plato, *Republic*, P. Shorey, trans. *The Collected Works of Plato*, E. Hamilton and H. Cairns, eds. (New Jersey: Princeton University Press, 1961), 382b. All subsequent references to Plato's texts will be taken from this volume, unless otherwise indicated.

With regard to the pertinence of Voegelin's analysis for the understanding of these phenomena, we require no more than a brief statement. Voegelin's philosophy of consciousness constitutes an attempt to clarify the true structure of consciousness in its relation to the divine. It is also an attempt to indicate the manner in which that structure manifests itself symbolically in the historical field. And finally, it develops a critical assessment of deformative theological types. Voegelin's analysis is thoroughly theological, for as he asserts, "True humanity requires true theology; the man with false theology is an untrue man" (*OH* III, 67).

The term "theology" sets the context for all major issues to be discussed in this work. Broadly stated, our analysis will move on the levels of both language and existence in order to clarify and critically assess several theological types of speech and their related states of consciousness. More specifically, our argument will begin with an exegesis of Voegelin's understanding of consciousness which, in turn, will form the basis of a critical discussion of three deformative types of symbolization prevalent in modernity.

In Chapter One, we will examine Voegelin's conception of the fundamental structures of consciousness and the manner in which these structures are manifested symbolically. The analysis will be primarily exegetical, attempting to develop an understanding of consciousness and symbolization that will serve as a measure against which the deformative types of symbolization discussed in Chapter Two might be tested. The primary texts to be considered are Voegelin's essay "Equivalences of Experience and Symbolization in History" and "The Beginning of the Beginning," the first chapter of *Order and History*, Volume V. Our discussion of the "Equivalences" paper will afford us a general insight into Voegelin's understanding of the process of symbolization as well as of the question of universality and symbolic difference. The exegesis of the chapter from *Order and History*, Volume V, will fill out this analysis by indicating more precisely the various modes of symbolization employed by consciousness and the corresponding structures they express. The principle symbolic forms to be considered are intentionality, luminosity, and reflective distance. In short, Chapter One of this book will constitute an attempt to articulate Voegelin's true *theologia*, that is, Voegelin's account of the true nature of consciousness in its relation to the divine.

As we have already indicated, Chapter Two is a critical analysis of several deformative types of symbolization prevalent in modern philosophical and religious discourse. The first to be discussed is the problem of subjectivism and symbolic difference. The central thrust of the subjectivist's position is the claim that "all men are not the same," that human experience is not universal, but conditioned by subjective factors, linguistic or otherwise, which vary from person to person. The difficulty with the position is to be found in its denial of the notion of "universal humanity," an idea which lies at the heart of both Voegelin's and Plato's understanding of theology. In response, our argument is an attempt to show how the subjectivist conception of linguistic forms as the expression of radically individuated private experience is incapable of accounting for the phenomenon of language itself. Stated positively, we argue that the fact of linguistic communication is intelligible only on the assumption of a deep commonality with regard to the structure of human consciousness.

The second issue to be addressed in this chapter is that of dogma and the loss of symbolic meaning. According to Voegelin, the meaning of a symbol is derived from the experience of reality that engendered it. Once the symbol is understood (or, rather, misunderstood) as a concept independent of the experience, it is emptied of its meaning. This is the problem of dogma. Language symbols are emptied of their meaning through their separation from engendering experiences and, in turn, are given new meanings or are pronounced meaningless, depending on one's response to the initial deformation. In order to bring this deformative use of language into analytic clarity, we will develop our analysis concretely through a critical examination of Feuerbach's psychology of projection and, by way of contrast, an exegesis of Plato's notion of the "living word" in the Egyptian Tale of the *Phaedrus*.

The third and final matter to be discussed in Chapter Two is the notion of "pneumopathology." The term itself is Schelling's, although it refers recognizably to the same phenomena as Plato's *nosos* (disease) and *anoia* (scary ignorance), as well as the Hebrew *nabal* (foolishness) and Cicero's *morbus animi* (diseased soul). It is intended to be descriptive of a discipline that analyses deformative states of consciousness, states of consciousness that, among other things, result in improper speech concerning the gods.

According to Voegelin, one of the most telling ways in which such disturbances of the soul manifest themselves is through the prohibition of questioning, and in particular the prohibition of the Question concerning the divine ground of being. This prohibition is necessitated by the fact that a thinker whose existence is no longer ordered by the erotic movement toward the divine ground of being will necessarily have to deny, if not eliminate, all symbolic forms that challenge his constricted state of existence. Our analysis will centre around a discussion of the work of two thinkers who advocate this prohibition: Karl Marx and Richard Rorty.

In keeping with the general thrust of the discussion, we will not simply engage in arguments concerning the symbolic deformations, but will attempt to indicate more precisely the *nosos* of the soul that produces such symbols. The descriptive terms that emerge through this analysis are notions such as hubris, *pleonexia* (greed), and *libido dominandi* (mad desire), for what unites such apparently disparate thinkers as Marx and Rorty is their shared Promethean hatred of the gods--Rorty through his repudiation of wisdom and Marx through his desire to possess it absolutely.

In the Conclusion, we will attempt to articulate and answer two questions that arise in response to this analysis. These questions can be stated as follows: (1) How does one move from a state of disorder, i.e., from a false theology, to a true state of existence, i. e., a state constituted by a proper response to the divine? and (2) How is this true state established as true? The former question pertains to the notion of education, while the latter pertains to the problem of proof.

In response to the first question, our discussion will be guided by Voegelin's analysis of Plato's term *periagoge* (turning around). The analysis of this term is particularly appropriate in the context of this work, for it indicates that the movement from falsehood to truth is not merely a matter of language, but of the "turning around" of one's whole soul, of a reorientation of one's existence. Furthermore, it points up the fact that this truth is not something that must be added to consciousness--something not already present, but a form of existence that is the potential of all human beings.

Concerning the second question, our analysis will centre around Voegelin's discussion of Anselm's *Proslogion* in his paper "Quod Deus Dicitur." Here we will attempt to clarify the nature of proof, its various forms, and the dimensions of existence in which these forms are applicable and those in which they are not. Essential to this discussion will be an examination of Voegelin's claim that "one cannot prove reality by a syllogism" (*QDD*, 579), a claim that is based on the distinction between *apodeixis* (proof as a logical demonstration) and *epideixis* (proof as pointing).

_____

CHAPTER ONE

SYMBOLIZATION AND THE STRUCTURE OF CONSCIOUSNESS

1. Symbolization and Equivalence

In his paper "Equivalences of Experience and Symbolization in History," Voegelin engages in a meditative search for the constants of human order as revealed in the historical movements of consciousness, constants that reveal themselves as a content. The search necessarily involves an analysis of the symbols that man has employed throughout history in his attempt to articulate his experience of reality. Some philosophers of history assume that the *telos* of such a search is the discovery of a set of propositions concerning right order, a set of dogmas that denote substantively the true order of existence. Thus understood, the search, when fulfilled, would circumvent itself; it would be the search to end all searching. Voegelin claims that any such attempt is doomed to fail, for when one approaches the historical field in this way, one does not find a constant manifesting itself as a content, but rather a series of rival forms of symbolization, "each claiming to be the only true one, but none of them commanding the universal acceptance it demands in the name of truth" (*EESH*, 217). "Far from discovering the permanent values of existence," one will rather "find [oneself] lost in the noisy struggle among the possessors of dogmatic truth--theological, or metaphysical, or ideological" (Ibid.). Faced with this spectacle, one might consider it the better part of wisdom simply to abandon the enterprise altogether and, as Voegelin suggests, become "an honest relativist and historicist" (Ibid.).

Voegelin is indeed in sympathy with such an analysis. However, he claims that what is true in this sceptical analysis is lost when it embraces relativism as the only plausible alternative. The reason for this is that relativism, while it ostensibly rejects the substantive claims of the possessors of wisdom, actually accepts their fundamental assumption that if truth *is*, it must be a matter of "permanent values" or propositions correctly denoting the order of reality.[3] This is what gives relativism its sense: it despairs of an answer precisely because an answer is what it expects. The difficulty with relativism, then, is not that its sceptical analysis is too radical, but that it is not radical enough. If one were to push the analysis further and reject, not only the content of the various attempts to articulate the truth of reality propositionally, but also the conception of truth that makes such attempts intelligible, one could preserve the sceptical critique of dogmatic truth while avoiding the equally deformative rejection of truth *per se*.

Two insights follow from these remarks. First, whatever the constants in human history may be, they are not propositional statements concerning true order. As Voegelin states, this is due to the fact that "existence does not have the structure of order, or for that matter, of disorder, but the structure of a tension between truth and deformation of reality" (*EESH*, 220). Second, the apprehension of this tensional structure--the gaining of true understanding--is contingent on the way in which one approaches the phenomena, i.e., the order of one's own existence. As we have seen, if one approaches the historical field with "the belief that the truth of existence is a set of propositions concerning the

---

[3]There is also another sense in which relativism is like dogmatic absolutism. Those who endorse relativism often claim that the position is superior because, in a world of dogmatic ideologues, it offers a theoretical basis for openness. Yet, once the search for a common truth has been abandoned, the very notion of tolerance or openness is undermined. One need not be tolerant of another person's view, for presumably that view, in terms of its truth, is no more "correct" or "legitimate" than one's own. Here the existential basis for true openness is lost. For an interesting discussion of this matter, see Allan Bloom, *The Closing of the American Mind* (New York: Simon and Schuster, 1987), 39-41.

right order of man in society and history," the field itself becomes unintelligible, it becomes a field of competing conceptions of truth and order with no unifying structure.

The first inference above concerns the nature of existence itself, its structure, constancy, and symbolization; the second pertains to the question of how one comes to understand that structure, given the apparently circular nature of understanding, that is, that one must live in the truth before one can understand it, and that one must understand it before one can come to live in it. The latter question will occupy us presently; at this point, however, we must concentrate on the first inference.

As we have noted, Voegelin rejects the idea that the truth of reality, in terms of its content, can either be propositionally circumscribed or be possessed absolutely by human consciousness. As he writes, "ultimate doctrines, systems and values" concerning the nature of reality are "phantasmata engendered by deformed existence" (*EESH,* 217). The impossibility of propositional representation is due to the structure of existence itself, and Voegelin describes the structure of existence as having the character of the "In-Between, of the Platonic *metaxy*" (Ibid.).

By the analytic term *metaxy*, Voegelin indicates that consciousness is existentially constituted by its place "In-Between" human existence in bodily form and the non-spatial and non-temporal divine ground of being. That is, the term *metaxy* points up the fact that man is neither a beast nor a god, but something between the two. This "In-Between" structure of existence is revealed through many of the symbols that man has employed throughout history. Among such symbols are these sets: "life and death, immortality and mortality, perfection and imperfection, truth and untruth, sense and senselessness of existence" (Ibid.). If anything is a "constant in the history of mankind, i.e, in the time dimension of existence," it is the "structure of consciousness itself" (Ibid.). As Voegelin, states, "Regarding this constant structure certain propositions can indeed be advanced" (Ibid.). It will be advantageous at this point to list the propositions in their entirety, for they constitute the matrix of the discussion that follows:

> 1) Man participates in the process of reality. The implications of the fundamental proposition, then, can be expressed by the following propositions:

2) Man is conscious of reality as a process, of himself as being part of reality, and of his consciousness as a mode of participation in its process.

3) While consciously participating, man is able to engender symbols which express his experience of reality, of himself as the experiencing agent, and of his conscious experiencing as the action and passion of participating.

4) Man knows the symbols engendered to be part of the reality they symbolize-- the symbols consciousness, experience, and symbolization denote the area where the process of reality becomes luminous to itself. To the positive statements we, finally, can add three corollaries of a cautionary nature:

5) Reality is not a given that could be observed from a vantage point outside itself but embraces the consciousness in which it becomes luminous.

6) The experience of reality cannot be total but has the character of a perspective.

7) The knowledge of reality conveyed by the symbols can never become a final possession of truth, for the luminous perspectives that we call experiences, as well as the symbols engendered by them, are part of reality in process (*EESH,* 221).

We will discuss these propositions in turn.

Regarding the claims of the first proposition, the most obvious implication is that there is, indeed, a reality in which human consciousness exists, a reality which, although not wholly "other" than consciousness, is recognized as extending beyond its limits, both in terms of knowledge and being. Simply put, in order to participate in something, there must, in fact, be something there in which to participate. Conversely, one cannot participate in reality if reality *is* merely a projection, linguistic or otherwise, of one's own consciousness. Here, the best one could manage would be a playful rearranging of the images thrown up by consciousness. Once the real is understood as an imaginative projection of consciousness, the notion of "participation" becomes senseless. Man no longer expresses, through the symbols of consciousness, his participatory role in reality; rather, he *creates* it.

Furthermore, the notion of participation indicates a certain reciprocity between consciousness and reality. Consciousness is not an autonomous subject that relates itself to reality solely through the denotative function of intentional linguistic signs. This form of intentionalism, prevalent among modern linguistic philosophers, eclipses the reality of participation; it conceives reality as an external thing to which consciousness relates itself exclusively on the level of intentionality. Philosophy, in this sense, is nothing more than epistemology, or a *theory of knowledge*. The relation of consciousness to reality becomes a question, not of being, but of correct representation within the framework of a semantic theory of truth; in other words, it becomes a question of whether the images of a subjective consciousness accurately reflect reality as it obtains independently of that consciousness.

Thus understood, the question of the participatory function of existential consciousness in reality becomes senseless. Human existence is structurally consigned to the role of spectator. Consciousness is no longer a partner in the community of being, but a non-participatory presence that assumes the merely secondary function of reflecting the structure of the primary realm of being--in this view, the external world. Given this conception of consciousness and reality, the meaning of human existence becomes tenuous indeed. One is even tempted to wonder, with Occam, whether it might in fact be "vain to do with more what can be done with fewer."

The notion of process in Voegelin's first proposition does not denote a movement of reality that will come to its conclusion in the immanent order of space and time. Voegelin is neither a Hegelian nor a liberal. He does not believe either that the process of reality can be cognitively comprehended by consciousness or that it can be realized, in terms of its End, in a concrete form of political organization.[4] Rather, the process, as it manifests itself in consciousness, is experienced as a movement toward a dimension of reality beyond the spatio-temporal world, a dimension of reality that will never be

---

[4]For an interesting discussion of the charge that Voegelin himself is something of a Hegelian, see Thomas Altizer's paper "A New History and a New but Ancient God," *Journal of the American Academy of Religion*, XLIII, (1975), 757-64. See also Eric Voegelin, "Response to Professor Altizer's 'A New History and a New but Ancient God,'" *Journal of the American Academy of Religion*, XLIII, (1975), 765-72.

drawn within the limited scope of human understanding and action. The movement of the process of reality is toward a *telos* out of time rather than one that obtains in time.

Voegelin's second proposition indicates that man can become aware of his place in reality, that his participation in reality is not blind, but reflectively present to consciousness. His third proposition reveals that it is precisely this awareness of the experience of participation that is reflected in the symbols thrown up by consciousness. Moreover, the content of these symbols affords us insight into three different dimensions of reality: (1) they express man's experience of reality, i.e., his understanding of the nature of reality; (2) they indicate that this experience is always from the perspective of man; and (3) they articulate the structure of consciousness itself by reflectively expressing the nature of its experience of participation in the process of reality.

The insight of the fourth proposition is that, insofar as symbols are part of the reality they symbolize, they do not constitute an autonomous realm. The symbols are just as much a part of reality as consciousness is; thus, if consciousness experiences its existence as tensional, as characterized by the Platonic *metaxy*, then the symbols themselves, if they are to express that experience faithfully, cannot be understood independently of that tension. The importance of this understanding of symbols is that it prohibits any linguistic transcendentalism, or the view that language is a system of signs, unaffected by the structure of existence, which can be used to refer to that structure from some place outside or beyond it. For if symbols are part of reality, then the notion of a linguistic vantage point outside reality becomes senseless. Language can express one's experience of reality, but it cannot transcend that experience.

Voegelin's final propositions serve to caution against certain misunderstandings to which the first four are susceptible by making explicit the perspectival nature of consciousness' understanding of reality. First, they indicate that man's understanding of reality is limited by the fact that man himself is a part of that reality. His knowledge is never from the standpoint of one who is "outside" reality but always from his place "within" it.

Further, this notion of "place" implies that man's experience of reality is not "total but has the character of a perspective." In the context of Voegelin's work, however, "the term *perspective* must not be understood in a subjective sense" (*Anamnesis*, 164). Voegelin rejects the idea that "there is a multitude of perspectives," that man's experience of reality is conditioned by radically individuated subjective factors. Rather, according to Voegelin there is "only one perspective," a perspective that holds in the case of all men and that is "determined by the place of man in reality" (Ibid.).

Finally, given that man is merely a part of reality, and that reality is experienced as a process, it follows that man can never gain a comprehensive understanding of reality. As Voegelin asserts, "the knowledge of reality conveyed by the symbols can never become a final possession of truth, for the luminous perspectives we call experiences, as well as the symbols engendered by them, are part of reality in process" (*EESH*, 221). In this sense, the meaning of existence, from the perspective of human understanding, *always remains a mystery*, even if the structure of that mystery can be analytically clarified.

Voegelin's analysis, as he himself is aware, is "bound to arouse misgivings." The most significant misgiving may be the problem of subjectivism. The fact that consciousness' "cognition of participation...is not directed toward an object of the external world," but is the manner in which consciousness expresses "the experience of its own structure" immediately invites certain questions concerning both the universality and the truth of the analysis. Voegelin himself articulates several of them:

> Can we really speak of a constant structure of existence and assume the propositions to express it adequately? Are not the symbols employed admittedly part of the structure they are supposed to express? Is there really any such structure apart from the imagery of the propositions? Are they more than an attempt, inevitably futile, to escape from a process from which, as they state themselves, man cannot escape? (Ibid., 222).

.

In response, Voegelin asserts that although the propositions are self-reflective, this act of self-reflection is real.[5] It is an attempt on the part of consciousness to articulate its own concrete structure, a structure manifest in its symbolic movements. It is not, however, an attempt *to escape that structure*. The process of reality cannot be escaped. The propositions that emerge through the act of reflection can do no more than raise into consciousness the role it plays in the process.

Might one not insist that although the propositions express the real movements of, say, Voegelin's consciousness, this does not imply that they do so with regard to the consciousness of all men? Voegelin removes himself from this form of subjectivism by asserting that, while the truth of the propositions is, indeed, found in the conscious experience of one man, "it is recognizably related to a less reflected experience of participation and its less differentiated symbolization" (*EESH*, 222). The content of this recognition is that the propositions, although affording us a more differentiated insight into the structure of consciousness, are "equivalents of the symbols which have been found unsatisfactory and whose want of differentiation has motivated the effort of reflection" (Ibid.). How is this so?

Through a shift in experience, or the advent of a more differentiated awareness of consciousness' structure, there results a dissatisfaction with the symbols hitherto employed. Consciousness then sets about trying to find a more adequate form of symbolization, one that will reflect linguistically the newly differentiated experience. In the confrontation between these newly formed symbols and the preceding ones, there occurs the recognition of a relation of equivalence between them, for although the new symbolization indicates a deeper insight into the nature of reality, the reality newly

---

[5]An important feature of Voegelin's work is his broad empiricism, i.e., his willingness to consider the reality of human experience as it presents itself to consciousness. Against this position there are those who argue that such experiences are not real, but illusory. For an interesting discussion of Voegelin's response to this charge, see Eric Voegelin, "Immortality: Experience and Symbol," *Harvard Theological Review*, 60:3, (1960), 252-53.

understood remains recognizably the same. This recognition renders the charge of subjectivism untenable, for it points up a continuity of experience that makes understanding possible, even in the presence of different symbolic forms--that is,recognition implies understanding, and the phenomenon of understanding suggests that experience is not radically individuated, but common to all human beings.

Despite the fact that this commonality or constant is a necessary element of understanding, we have still not indicated precisely where it is to be found, that is, we are still faced with these questions: In what sense can the symbols be said to be equivalent? What is the constant that persists through the various symbolic forms and justifies, in spite of their "phenomo-typical" differences, the relation of equivalence between them? The constant is not to be found in the symbols themselves, for, as we have indicated, the symbols, taken on their own, constitute not a unified historical field but a "heterogeneous" and, at times, seemingly "incommensurable" series of rival linguistic forms. Where, then, is the constant to be found?

Voegelin's first response to the problem is as follows: "The sameness which justifies the language of 'equivalences' does not lie in the symbols themselves but in the experiences which have engendered them" (*EESH,* 215). However, as Voegelin's analysis unfolds, it begins to appear as though the experiences themselves are not quite as constant as this remark suggests, for, as we have indicated elsewhere, different symbolic forms are different precisely because they are engendered by different types of experience. For example, Hegel's claim at the end of the *Phenomenology* to have achieved the epistemological perspective of the Divine reflects the consciousness of one who has lost contact with the experience of the divine mystery. However, Hegel's claim, deformative as it may be, is nonetheless a "true" expression of Hegel's experience, that is to say, the deformative symbols in which he expresses his claim adequately reflect the deformative experience. The experience, then, cannot be the constant for which we are looking, and this for two reasons. The first is the simple fact that, as we have just indicated, experiences differ. The second relates to another aspect of Voegelin's analysis, however, one which we observed in our discussion of the tensional structure of consciousness and the notion of perspective.

According to Voegelin, human consciousness is structurally constituted by the role it plays in reality, by its mode of participation. The specific character of its participation is described in the Platonic symbol of the *metaxy*. Man is neither a god nor a beast, but something between the two. Furthermore, man recognizes this role or place through symbols thrown up by consciousness in its attempt to articulate its structure linguistically. Among these symbols, the type essential for this recognition points to a divine reality that transcends temporal existence; it expresses an erotic longing in the human spirit for that which is beyond it. Through these symbols, consciousness recognizes its own finitude, both existentially and epistemologically. Existence must always remain a mystery, for reality, at its deepest level, is unknowable to man.

A difficulty seems to arise from this analysis. Voegelin must find a constant in order to justify the language of equivalents, yet the constant cannot manifest itself substantively in consciousness, either on the level of symbolization or on the level of experience, for this would contradict the insight that consciousness' understanding of reality is always perspectival and always limited by the ineffability of the divine ground.

In response to this difficulty, Voegelin tells us that "the constant that will justify the language of equivalent experiences and symbols must be sought on a level deeper than the level of equivalent experiences which engender equivalent symbols" (*EESH*, 224). Regarding the nature or character of this "deeper level," Voegelin--following Heraclitus, Aeschylus, and Plato--offers the notion of the "depth of the psyche." The depth of the psyche does not "furnish a substantive content in addition" to our experiences of the various dimensions of reality, that is, our experiences of "God, man, the world, and society, and of existential tension, and of participation" (Ibid., 225). It stands in continuity with consciousness: "There is neither an autonomous consciousness nor an autonomous depth but only a consciousness in continuity with its own depth" (Ibid., 230). In times "when the light of truth has dimmed and its symbols are losing their credibility," it is a place from which consciousness can "drag up" new insights concerning the nature of reality. But the depth, in terms of its content, always remains below or beyond conscious experience. As Voegelin asserts, "there is a psyche deeper than consciousness, and there is a reality deeper than reality experienced, but there is no consciousness deeper than consciousness" (Ibid., 226).

One may still want to ask precisely what dimension of reality, "in terms of the primordial field", (the community of God, man, the world, society), "is touched when man descends into the depth of his psyche" (Ibid., 227). According to Voegelin, since the new "truth hauled up from the depth effects the perspectival view of the [primordial] field as a whole, he will not identify the reality of the depth with any of the partners in the community but with the underlying reality that makes them partners in a common order, i.e., with the substance of the Cosmos" (*EESH*, 227). Stated simply, "the depth of the psyche below consciousness is the depth of the Cosmos below the primordial field," that is, "the *anima mundi*" (Ibid., 228).

A cautionary word is in order here, for, as Voegelin asserts, the *anima mundi* (the world soul) "has badly suffered from its deformation into a 'metaphysical concept' and its doctrinal use as part of a philosophical tradition" (Ibid). The term "world soul" is *not* the symbolic articulation of an *experience*: "We have no experience of the depth of the Cosmos as psyche" (Ibid.). Rather, it is the term Plato coined in the context of a myth in order to account for the "depth of the soul." The myth "articulates neither the experience of the primordial field, nor the experience of the psyche, but achieves the imaginative fusion of insights gained from the two types of experience separately" (Ibid., 228).

With regard to the truth of the myth, Plato, in the *Timaeus*, wavered between two descriptions of it: "the more assertive *alethinos logos* (true story) and the more doubtful *eikos mythos* (likely myth)" (*Ibid.*). This tentativeness, Voegelin writes, derives from Plato's awareness that "the *psyche* and *logos* of man" are no more than "kindred (*syngenes*)" to "the divine *psyche* and *logos* of the Cosmos" (Ibid.). Plato, it would appear, was clear-headed enough to avoid the overexuberant conclusions of those thinkers who have, ever since antiquity, wanted to replace the notion of kindredness with the definitive relation of synonymy. Unlike Hegel, Plato refused to identify himself "with the World-Soul unfolding its Logos" (Ibid.).

In our concrete attempts to symbolically articulate our understanding of reality, we often experience a dissatisfaction with the symbols we have at our disposal. We feel that the symbols employed by our ancestors to articulate their understanding and experience of reality cannot articulate our own. In this situation, we are faced with the rather arduous task of trying to find a new symbolic form that more adequately reflects our experience. A particular historical instance of this relation between dissatisfaction and search can be found in Plato's response to Homer. When confronted with the "unseemly" Homeric symbolization of divine reality, Plato found himself in the position of having to develop a new form of symbolization. In Plato's case, this task was in part accomplished by his use of the preposition "beyond" (*epekeina*) as descriptive of the divine; "the good itself is not essence but still transcends essence in dignity and surpassing power" (*Rep*, 509b).

The point of our present analysis, however, is to discuss not the specific nature of a given symbolic advance but the notion of symbolic advance or movement itself. It is through the symbolic movements we perceive in the historical field that the process in the depth is recognized.

Our argument runs as follows: Linguistic symbols express states of consciousness. There is therefore a continuity between experience and language. However, the notion of continuity does not imply a closed relation; it does not, as the historicist would have us believe, imply that experience and its symbolic manifestation constitute the limits of consciousness' access to reality. The experience cannot be absolute, because human existence is characterized by the phenomenon of dissatisfaction, a phenomenon that suggests there is something in consciousness by means of which it is able to recognize both deficiency and superiority with regard to various forms of experience and symbolization. This "something" cannot be experience itself, for it is experience that such dissatisfaction calls into question. Insofar as the experience of dissatisfaction is relational in character, experience cannot, taken on its own, produce it; something more is required.

It might be argued that this "something more" is not something *other* than experience, that it is not a deeper dimension of human existence, but simply an *additional* experience of reality, one that consciousness cannot account for within the limits of its present experience. However, such a response begs the question, for what is at issue is precisely consciousness' ability to recognize a "new" or "additional" experience. The fact of symbolic change--of the advent of new insights and the rejection of old ones, and of new, more comprehensive experiences of reality--points to the reality of the depth of the psyche, the reality from which these new insights emerge. Moreover, it indicates that the depth of the psyche, although discerned in the experiential and symbolic movements in the historical field, can itself never become part of that field.

> We experience psyche as consciousness that can descend into the depth of its own reality, and the depth of the psyche as reality that can rise to consciousness, but we do not experience a content of the depth other than the content that has entered consciousness (*EESH*, 227).

With the descent into the depth, our "journey" or "search" has come to its end. As Voegelin states, "there is a depth below consciousness, but there is no depth below depth in infinite regress" (Ibid., 230). Having thus arrived, however, we still have not found "a constant manifesting itself in its content," for given that the depth "renders no truth but the equivalent experiences of the primordial field of reality, the search for a substantive constant of history that would be exempt from the status of an equivalent must be dismissed as fallacious" (Ibid). Even with the discovery of the depth, we have not uncovered an "ultimate" or "absolute" truth of reality. And "since no such apocalyptic truth of reality behind reality can be experienced, we must draw the consequence and," as Voegelin asserts, "push the equivalence of symbols, that we have already extended to the experiences engendering them, still further back to the depth by which the experience lives" (Ibid.).

By extending the relation of equivalence into the depth, Voegelin's analysis successfully undermines the penchant for an absolute perspective, i.e., the symbolic articulation of a constant in history revealing itself in its content. However, in so doing, it also seems to undermine the possibility of finding a constant that will justify the "language of equivalent experiences and symbols," for the depth, now understood to be merely equivalent, was originally said to be precisely this "constant" (Ibid., 224).

The solution to this dilemma is to be found by understanding aright the true nature of the depth and the insight it affords us with regard to the structure of human existence. The recognition of the depth indicates that consciousness is characterized by a "process of search," a process whereby reality is perceived as moving toward its truth in the case of human consciousness. Through consciousness' experience of the emergence of new truth from the depth, it recognizes itself as structurally constituted through its participation in the process of reality. Hence, what we find through an analytic descent into the depth is not a constant manifesting itself as an absolute content, but only "the constancy of a process" (*EESH*, 233).

2. Three Structures of Consciousness

The preceding remarks outline Voegelin's understanding of the nature of consciousness and the process whereby it manifests itself symbolically in the historical field. What remains to be discussed in greater detail are the various types of symbolic forms that consciousness employs to articulate itself and the corresponding structures of which the forms are an expression. In the present section, we will analyse what Voegelin identifies as three distinct structures of consciousness: intentionality, luminosity, and reflective distance. The discussion will proceed in this manner for the following reason. As we noted previously, the constant structure of consciousness, which legitimates the claim of universality, is not a set of propositions that reveal substantively the truth of reality. Rather, what is constant in human existence is a process--a "quest" or "search"--

whereby consciousness, through a meditative descent into its depth, attempts to find a new linguistic form that will optimally symbolize its experience of reality. This process, when most clearly articulated, reveals itself as consciousness' search for the ground of its existence, a search through which consciousness attempts to find a Beginning beyond all finite beginnings in space and time. Through this search, consciousness also discovers the nature of its own being. In other words, the quest affords us insight in two directions: (1) It illuminates the structure of reality as experienced by man; and (2) it illuminates the structure of man himself as revealed through his search for the structure of reality. This, in fact, is a principle which lies at the heart of Voegelin's own investigations. Man discovers who he is through his quest for that which he is not. The two forms of insight, paradoxical as they may seem, constitute the unified structure of the quest. With regard to our present endeavour, we too must begin with just such a search, a search for the Beginning, because the structures of consciousness that are our present concern will be illuminated through it.

a) The Search for the Beginning

In Search of Order, the fifth and final volume of *Order and History*, opens with an analysis of certain problems of Beginning. Voegelin initiates this discussion by means of a reflective inquiry concerning the notion of a beginning *per se*. He wonders whether the present work's opening sentence, which he has just completed, is actually the beginning it purports to be, i.e., the beginning of a chapter that will constitute an expression of the author's meditative quest for an adequate response to the question of the Beginning. The sentence, indeed, is finished and, hence, appears to constitute such a beginning. Yet, from the point of view of the reader, can it really be so until the chapter as a whole has been read, until one can judge whether the sentence, in terms of its content, is truly the beginning of the chapter in which it occurs? Moreover, the question stands for the author as well. Voegelin "knows from experience that new ideas have a habit of emerging while the writing is going on, compelling changes in the construction and making the beginning unsuitable" (*OH* V, 13). It would seem that "the story has no beginning before it has come to its end." We are therefore faced with the question: which comes first, "the beginning or the end?" (Ibid.)

Voegelin does not let the analysis conclude with this paradoxic response, but refers us to a further phenomenon, the "chapter," understood as the whole that encompasses the paradoxic tension. Is the chapter, with its spatial, temporal, and cognitive dimensions, that which comes first? No, for although a complete literary unit, it does not stand on its own but has its meaning through the role it plays in a larger whole, a book. However, the book is not the beginning we are seeking either; it is merely

> an event in a vast social field of thought and language, of writing and reading about matters which the members of the field believe to be of concern for their existence in truth. The whole is no beginning in an absolute sense; it is no beginning of anything at all unless it has a function in a communion of existential concern; and the communion of concern as a social field depends for its existence on the communicability of the concern through language (*OH* V, 13).

With these remarks we are led back, through notions such as "communion of existential concern," "social field," and "communicability," to the question of language. And here Voegelin pauses: might the word have been in the Beginning after all? For Voegelin this is no more than a pause, for he knows well enough that language, although necessary for communication in a social field, does not constitute an end of the quest which would be intelligible as its Beginning.[6]

At this point we would do well to mention a possible derailment of the quest which has become quite pervasive in certain modern philosophical schools. Those with a penchant for linguistic analysis consider the quest to be over when they arrive at the phenomenon of language. There are no beginnings left to explore; language *is*, it is

---

[6]This remark is not intended to be a criticism of the Johanine myth of Christ as the formative beginning of creation. With such a myth Voegelin would, I think, be sympathetic. Rather, the point of the remark is to criticize those who claim that reality is nothing more than the product of our symbolizing practices.

argued, the formative Beginning of reality, the author of creation.[7] In such a view, the complex relation of reality and language is reversed. Language, ceasing to be understood as an expressive event articulating consciousness' experience of a reality that stands beyond it as the ordering pole of its quest, is conceived as reality itself. The Beginning beyond time and space is replaced by a beginning that obtains within the purely immanent order of linguistic signs. The criterion by which this position is to be judged as a deformation is the quest itself. A detailed critique must therefore wait until we have explored more fully the question of the Beginning and the structures of consciousness and reality from which it emerges.

We return to our initial task: when, in our pursuit of a Beginning, we arrive at the phenomenon of language, we see that language itself is functionally diversified. Voegelin does not merely offer us a "piece of information about familiar objects in the external world," but is also attempting to "communicate an act of participation in the quest for truth" (*OH*, 14).

> Besides satisfying standards of intelligibility in the everyday sense of reference to objects, the language must be in common in the sense of communicating the meanings in the area of the existential quest; it must be able to convey the meanings of a philosopher's experience, meditation, and exegetic analysis (Ibid.).

Language conveys meaning on two distinct, but related, levels: it communicates meaning (1) by denotatively indicating objects in the spatio-temporal world, and (2) by symbolically articulating consciousness' quest for a truth of existence that transcends the realm of "things."

We know that language did not begin with the writing of Voegelin's book but has a history as the means by which human beings have communicated with one another regarding both of the aforementioned realms of being. The document presently under consideration is Voegelin's attempt to articulate his contribution to a quest for existential

---

[7]For a detailed discussion of this position, see Donald Davidson, "On the Very Idea of a Conceptual Scheme" and "True to the Facts" in his *Inquiries into Truth and Interpretation* (New York: Oxford University Press, 1984).

truth that has been unfolding ever since antiquity. The quest cannot be understood merely as a curious anomaly in the conscious experience of one man. Rather, it is an existential task under which humanity has laboured as far back as our historical records go. Given this dyadic structure of language and its historical continuity, Voegelin raises the question: "What is the structure in reality that will induce, when experienced, this equivocal use of the term 'language'?" (Ibid., 15)

Our analysis thus far has led us through a philosophical meditation on "certain problems of Beginning" to a question concerning the structure or type of reality that will produce, when experienced, the equivocal symbolic forms discovered through the process of the meditation. It has led us back to our original task of "rediscovering the experiences of consciousness and the language that will adequately express them." This being so, one might wonder about the fruitfulness of the preceding pages in that they have simply led us to the place we were before the analysis began. But are we in the same place? Upon reflection, it appears that the meditation has served to root our present endeavour in a concrete symbolic articulation of consciousness' experience of reality. We have come to the question of the structure of consciousness and its relation to reality, not as an idle philosophical preoccupation, but as a matter of existential concern, a concern firmly grounded in our experience of reality. Moveover, the quest for the Beginning, far from being merely a foil for the present analysis, will reveal itself in subsequent chapters as an essential dimension of our understanding of reality and as a basis of resistance against modern ideological deformations.

In response to the question: "What is the structure in reality that will induce, when experienced, this equivocal use of the term 'language'?" Voegelin asserts that the equivocal nature of language "is induced by the paradoxical structure of consciousness and its relation to reality" (*OH* V. 15). Under the first aspect of this paradox, consciousness assumes the place of a subject that, through the use of linguistic symbols, relates itself to reality as an *object intended*. Reality "assumes a metaphorical touch of external thingness" in relation to consciousness, understood as a subject located in bodily existence (Ibid.). Voegelin refers to "this structure of consciousness as its intentionality, and the corresponding structure of reality its thingness" (Ibid.). To this thingness Voegelin has given the technical name "thing-reality."

These structures constitute only one dimension of the paradox under consideration. Along with consciousness in its mode of intentionality--a bodily located consciousness opposed to reality as a thing--"we know the bodily located consciousness to be also real; and this concretely located consciousness does not belong to another genus of reality, but is part of the same reality that has moved, in its relation to man's consciousness, into the position of a thing" (Ibid.). Thus understood, reality becomes, not an object intended by consciousness, but the reality in which consciousness occurs "as an event of participation between partners in the community of being" (Ibid.). Consciousness "moves to the position of a predicative event in the subject reality as it becomes *luminous* for its truth" (Ibid.; emphasis mine). In its structure of luminosity, consciousness is the place where the comprehending reality, a reality to which Voegelin has given the technical name "It-reality," becomes luminous for its structure.

From our analysis, consciousness emerges as something having two structures, that of intentionality and that of luminosity, and corresponding to these respective structures, reality assumes the position of either (1) an object intended by consciousness, i.e., "thing-reality," or (2) the comprehending something in which consciousness occurs as a predicative event, i.e., "It-reality." We must now examine in more detail the nature of these structures in order to determine their significance for the question of the Beginning.

b) Intentionality and Luminosity

In its mode of intentionality, consciousness assumes the position of a subject intending reality as an object, i.e., as a thing. Now, it should be stated that this intentional stance, although only one dimension of consciousness' paradoxic structure, is not inherently deformative. It is a legitimate mode of cognition, perfectly suited to the area of reality in which the appropriate corresponding structures predominate. It is a legitimate mode of cognition in the physical sciences, for example. One would hardly consult a mystic philosopher if one wanted to calculate the forces in each truss in the designing of a suspension bridge. Difficulties arise, however, when this intentional mode of consciousness is taken as exhaustive for our understanding of reality, when, for example, the methods of the mathematizing sciences come to be understood as the exclusive means whereby the truth of reality can be discerned. If such a view is accepted, reality revealed in the luminous symbols of consciousness will be eclipsed. This, of course, is not to say that the philosopher's analysis of luminous language is imprecise or convoluted. Such an analysis is capable of clearly articulating the nature of the reality which is its concern. However, it must do so within the limits inherent to the paradoxic structure of that reality. To attempt to eliminate or resolve the paradox would result in a deformation of the reality being investigated. As Voegelin has said on numerous occasions, the "linguistic ambiguities" of Plato's analysis "are not caused by some negligence in [his] thought or writing" (*OH* V, 92); rather, they reflect the paradoxic structure of the reality to which his analysis applies.

The impetus for this deformation of luminous symbols is rooted, as we have said, in a misplaced concentration on intentionality. Consider the example of the symbol "the gods." Once the gods are conceived as being-things modelled on the beings-things that exist in space and time, that is, once they are conceived as "objects" of intentional consciousness, the reality illuminated by the symbol is obscured and speech about it becomes impossible. Insofar as divine reality cannot be demonstrated by inductive or deductive argumentation--forms of argumentation operative in the mode of intentionality-- it can no longer be reasonably affirmed. Those theologians and philosophers since Descartes who have accepted the terms of the deformation and then have attempted to develop "proofs" for God's existence within its theoretical constraints have ultimately had to face the unpleasant fact of Kant's "antinomies." However, Kant's antinomies are in fact the logical consequence of this type of reasoning and, in this sense, are not unacceptable. The difficulty with the analysis comes earlier; it is the attempt to speak about the gods as if they were things.

This penchant for objectifying the meaning of luminous symbols is provoked by the paradoxic structures now under consideration. As Voegelin asserts, the difficulty is that "the questioner has to tell the story of his struggle for the unflawed order from his position in the flawed order of thingly existence; and he can tell it, therefore, only in the flawed language that speaks of non-things in the mode of things" (*OH* V, 102). In light of these remarks it would seem that part of the paradoxic structure of language and consciousness is that the meaning of luminous symbols is burdened by the fact that it must express the truth of luminous reality through the language of intentionality, and this paradoxic structure invites a question concerning the very possibility of maintaining a legitimate distinction between intentional and luminous language. Why is this so? If, in human discourse, luminous symbols have the surface appearance of intentional language, how are we to determine the *difference* between them? We can only hint at an answer because the requisite analysis necessary for a fuller response is something we will develop in Chapter Two.

The difficulty is resolved through an appeal to the empirical fact of the phenomenon of luminous language itself. Throughout human history man has employed such language in his philosophic and religious discourse as a means of expressing his experience of transcendence. And he has done so even if, at times, he has found the adequate articulation of its meaning a difficult task. Although the symbols that illuminate the experience of divine reality appear in sentences as subjects to which various characteristics or qualities are predicated, nonetheless, they have been understood by those who have uttered them as pointing to a "non-thingly" divine reality beyond the limits of the form of reality denoted by the intentional proposition. The very fact that the question we are presently considering can be raised at all lends credence to the idea that the distinction is indeed legitimate. In order to be articulated, the question itself must assume that the language is *meaningful*. Less than this would render the question as senseless as the linguistic form it wishes to challenge.

Although infrequently discussed by Voegelin's commentators, there is a further aspect of intentional consciousness that is essential to our understanding in order to ward off certain of the philosophical deformations to which we have already alluded. Fundamental to Voegelin's understanding of consciousness and its relation to the reality it experiences is the notion of "participation." Voegelin writes: "The center of consciousness I found to be the experience of participation, meaning thereby the reality of being in contact with reality outside myself" (*AR*, 72). The symbol "participation" indicates that consciousness is not merely a spectator--not something radically other than the reality it experiences--but an active partner in that reality. The notion of a reality "outside" consciousness, therefore, does not imply the existence of a "self-contained" reality with which consciousness' only contact is a non-participatory act of cognitive representation. Consciousness' experience of reality is constituted by its participation in reality. The experience "is neither in the subject nor in the world of objects but In-Between, and that means In-Between the poles of man and of the reality that he experiences" (Ibid., 73).

For this understanding of the nature of consciousness' experience of reality, Voegelin found confirmation both in the work on myth carried out by the members of the Chicago Oriental Institute and in William James's "Radical Empiricism." Concerning the former, the analysis was conducted under the category of "consubstantiality" (Ibid., 72). Simply stated: "If man were not consubstantial with the reality he experiences, he could not experience it" (*AR*, 72). Regarding the latter, what Voegelin found helpful in articulating his own understanding of consciousness' participatory experience of reality was James's notion of "pure experience." Against those who claim that experience is "indefeasibly dualistic in structure," James argues for the notion of "pure experience," an experience that, at the moment of its occurrence, is in neither the conscious subject nor the world of objects. According to James, pure experience is characterized by no such dualism, by no epistemological gap. "No dualism of being represented and representing resides in the experience *per se*. In its pure state, or when isolated, there is no self-splitting of it into consciousness and what the consciousness is 'of."[8]   In its immediacy, pure experience "is plain, unqualified actuality or existence, a simple *that*."[9]

Pure experience in William James's sense is what Voegelin refers to as the "something that lies between the subject and object of participation" (Ibid.). The spatial metaphor "In-Between" can be misleading, however. The term does not denote the existence of a third "thing" in between consciousness and reality; it is not simply a modified form of dualism. Rather, it points up what Voegelin has elsewhere referred to as the "wholeness" of the participatory experience (*EESH*, 232). The term "wholeness" indicates that the reality of consciousness in its experience of a reality outside itself *is* the reality of participation itself and nothing but that reality. Consciousness is what it is by virtue of its place in the broader reality in which it participates. Once it is removed from that reality, meaningful speech concerning the nature of consciousness becomes impossible. If, through an act of imagination, you disassociate consciousness and reality and then begin casting about for a way of rejoining the two, you will be faced with either the hopeless epistemological dilemma of how the former can have knowledge of the latter or the eclipsing of the reality of consciousness altogether. To abstract consciousness from reality in this way, that is, to ask what consciousness *is* in itself, is as senseless as to deny all the physical characteristics of a silver chalice and then to ask what the chalice *is* in itself. The conditions stipulated by the question make an intelligible answer impossible.

Consciousness is not a "thing," it is not an entity, and hence any attempt to conceive of it as such in order to determine its properties or its relations to other things will ultimately be disappointed. This, of course, is not to say that consciousness has no reality of its own. There is indeed a reality that we call consciousness. That reality, however, is rightly understood only in the context of its participation among the partners in the community of being. We can illustrate the matter as follows: The piece we call

---

[8]William James, "Does Consciousness Exist," in *Essays in Radical Empiricism*, F. Burkhardt, ed. (Massachusetts: Harvard University Press, 1976), 13.

[9]Ibid.

the "queen" has a certain role to play in the game of chess. It can be moved in either a straight line or diagonally and is not restricted in the number of squares it may traverse. However, the fact that it can be moved in this way is something that is determined by its place in the game as a whole, a game that is constituted by the possible movements of a number of other pieces. Among knights, rooks, bishops, and pawns, as well as in the relationships between them, the queen has its meaning, its reality. The queen, therefore, cannot exist apart from these pieces and their relationships; and similarly, the pieces cannot exist apart from the queen. Both the queen and the other pieces exist. The nature of their existence, however, is inseparable from the relationships among them. In an analogous way, consciousness is constituted by its place among the other members of the community of being. Consciousness, like the queen in a game of chess, certainly exists, yet its existence is not something it possesses unto itself but something it possesses only through its participation in the whole of reality.

There will be those who will want to insist that unless we can state explicitly what consciousness *is* in itself, our analysis will amount to just so much relativism. Our response is twofold. First, although we assert that the reality of consciousness is constituted by the role it plays among the other partners in reality, that its being is relative to those partners, it is false to suggest that we are thereby committed to relativism. One can indeed say universally "true" things about the game of chess, and in particular about the piece we call the "queen." Similarly, one can say universally "true" things about the nature of consciousness. The language of "truth" and "universality" is in no way prohibited by our analysis. What is prohibited is the idea that one can speak truthfully about the nature of consciousness without doing so in the context of the reality in which consciousness exists.

In back of the charge of relativism is the misplaced desire for reality to be univocal, i.e., the desire for the constituent parts of reality to be autonomous entities that are singularly either this or that. Consciousness, it is argued, cannot be what it is by virtue of its relationship to other dimensions of reality, for if this were so, there would be no one, single truth about its nature.

Interestingly, this metaphysical concern for singularity seldom arises with regard to the content of everyday speech. We frequently speak of objects as being both large and small, important and unimportant, useful and useless, depending on the context in which they are considered. No one is particularly concerned that this multiplicity of predicates will in any way undermine our ability to speak "truthfully" about such objects. With regard to consciousness, our speech is equally equivocal. In its mode of intentionality, consciousness is a "subject" that intends reality as a "thing." But as we will see presently, consciousness, being also real, can be understood as a predicative event in the subject reality. Consciousness is both, because it is neither one nor the other. Our paradoxic speech about the structure of consciousness belies neither a mistake in reasoning nor the acceptance of some form of relativism. Rather, it results from the attempt to articulate the nature of consciousness as it participates in reality along with the other partners in the community of being.

The second part of our response is as follows: both Voegelin and James admit that in our everyday discourse, we do speak both about external objects and consciousness as a subject that cognitively apprehends such objects. Neither James nor Voegelin wishes to deny the legitimacy of this type of speech. James states that the dualism connoted by terms such as "thought and thing ... is still preserved in [his] account, but reinterpreted, so that, instead of being mysterious and elusive, it becomes verifiable and concrete."[10] The attributes of subjectivity and objectivity are realized "only when the experience is 'taken,' i.e., 'talked of,' twice, considered along with its two different contexts respectively."[11] Following James, Voegelin asserts that the "*pure experience* is the something that can be put into the context either of the subject's stream of consciousness or of objects in the external world" (*AR*, 72). What both Voegelin and James want is for

---

[10]Ibid., 7.

[11]Ibid., 13.

the language of subject and object to be properly understood. According to Voegelin, the poles of subject and object, the poles of the participatory pure experience, must not be hypostasized so as to denote two "self-contained entities" (Ibid., 73). The poles of the experience do indeed exist, but their existence is something that is mutually constituted by their participation in one another and in the broader reality that encompasses them. If the metaxic constitution of the pure experience is not kept in mind, one soon falls prey to one or the other of the epistemological dilemmas to which we have already alluded.

What the preceding remarks point up is that even in its mode of intentionality, a mode in which reality is intended as a "thing," consciousness' experience of reality is characterized by a sort of "in-betweenness." The fact that Voegelin understands intentional experience in this way is further supported by his remarks on the subject in *Order and History*, Volume V. He states that "by its position as an object intended by a consciousness that is bodily located, reality itself acquires a *metaphorical touch of external thingness*" (*OH* V, 15; emphasis mine). The term "external" suggests the idea that reality is something "other than," or unrelated to, consciousness. This is the reason why Voegelin asserts that it is no more than "metaphorical." Consciousness' experience of reality is always metaxic, i.e., it is always an event of participation between consciousness and the reality it experiences.

Thing-reality, however, is not the only reality in which consciousness participates, and intentionality is not the only structure of consciousness. Consciousness can also be understood as participating in the "comprehending reality" in which objects and events, along with consciousness itself, occur. To denote this comprehending reality, Voegelin has coined the technical term "It-reality." It-reality "is not an object of consciousness but the something in which consciousness occurs as an event of participation between the partners in the community of being" (*OH* V, 15). As an event in It-reality, consciousness must be understood as belonging "not to man in his bodily existence, but to the reality in which man, the other partners to the community of being, and the participatory relations among them occur" (Ibid.). Consciousness, experienced as a predicative event in the comprehending It-reality, is the place where the It "becomes *luminous* for its truth" (Ibid.). The luminosity of consciousness, however, is not restricted to a certain class of experience. Any experienced event in the comprehending reality can be a luminous event. Consciousness' experience of the generation and destruction of objects can reveal something of the truth of It-reality. And consciousness' experience of itself as being in tension toward the divine can also illuminate the movements of the comprehending reality. Together, these experiences form the basis of our understanding of the It-reality as it moves formatively toward its truth.

In our search for a Beginning, we have discovered two different structures of consciousness, intentionality and luminosity, and, corresponding to these structures, two different dimensions of reality, thing-reality and It-reality. We have already discussed at some length the structure of intentionality and, along with it, reality in its mode of thingness. In what way, however, are we to characterize It-reality? How does the It-reality manifest itself, in terms of its structure, in the luminous experiences of consciousness?

Before we outline Voegelin's response to these questions, we must first ward off a possible misinterpretation. When we talk about luminous symbols and the way they manifest the structures and movement of It-reality, we are not engaged in the epistemological task of discerning how a subjective consciousness represents a reality external to it. This form of dualism, as we have already argued, is what Voegelin wishes to reject. It-reality is not an object opposed to consciousness as a subject, but the reality in which consciousness occurs. Consciousness is not other than reality, but reality manifesting itself in a particular form. The epistemological question is therefore misplaced when applied to luminous experiences and their symbolization, for the object necessary in order for such a question to have sense *does not exist*. There may indeed be a disparity between the "story the It wants to tell" and the stories told by man, a disparity between the movement of the It-reality and the way man participates in that reality; however, that is not a problem of representational epistemology, but of life.

In order to articulate the structure of the It-reality as experienced by consciousness, Voegelin refers us to a "concrete case," a literary document that displays the structures presently under consideration, the text of Genesis 1.

The document opens with the following statement: "In the beginning God created the heavens and the earth." As Voegelin asserts, "we can hardly come closer to the real beginning of anything than in an original act of creation" (*OH* V, 19). However, even here we are faced with certain questions: "But what is creation? and how does God proceed when he creates?" (Ibid.) The answer is forthcoming from the text itself; at Genesis 1:3 we read: "God spoke: Light be! Light became."[12] The evocative act of creation is an act whereby God calls something into existence by uttering its name. Again, however, the text raises several questions, questions such as "To whom are the divine commands addressed? and who is the God who addresses them? or what is that kind of reality where the spoken word evokes the structures of which it speaks?" (Ibid.) To these questions, Voegelin responds:

> The authors of Genesis 1, we prefer to assume, were human beings of the same kind as we are; they had to face the same kind of reality, with the same kind of consciousness, as we do; and when, in their pursuit of truth, they put down their words on whatever material, they had to raise, and to cope with, the same questions we confront when we put down our words. In the situation created by the question: what is that kind of reality where the spoken word evokes the structures of which it speaks? they had to find the language symbols that would adequately express the experience and structure of what I have called the It-reality (*OH* V, 19).

The remaining question is simply this: "How did they do it?" (Ibid.). The text offers the following answer: "The earth was waste and void; darkness was on the face of the deep; and the spirit [breath] of God was moving over the face of the water" (Ibid.). The It-reality is experienced by consciousness as a tensional reality characterized by the movement of a formative force that imposes order on an at least "passively resistant

---

[12]Throughout *OH* V, Voegelin uses the more literal Buber-Rosenzweig translation of the Hebrew Bible.

counterforce" (Ibid., 20). Clearly, the Beginning the author symbolizes is not his own consciousness, but the comprehending It-reality as it moves from a divine Beginning into the formation of an ordered thingly reality that is the structural differentiation of a formless waste.

The story reflects man's search for order and meaning in reality that transcends the disorder he experiences in his temporal existence, for a meaning in existence that, although revealed through the objects and events in the spatio-temporal world, including his own consciousness, is not exhausted by them. The story also reflects the tensional structure of the It-reality. Consciousness' quest for the Beginning becomes luminous both for the tensional structure of the It-reality and the structure of consciousness itself. The story of the quest must be understood as originating "neither in the temporal dimension of external objects nor in the dimension of eternity, of a divine time out of time, but somewhere in-between the two, in the dimension symbolized by Plato as the metaxy" (Ibid., 27).

This *metaxy* is certainly not the *metaxy* of intentional experience. Although the symbol can be appropriately applied to intentional experience, its principal use in Voegelin's work is to describe the In-Betweenness of consciousness' experience of the divine. The divine is not an object intended by a subjective consciousness. It is not a thing. To treat it as such would be to hypostasize the poles of the participatory pure experience; it would be to conceive the poles of the experience as if they were "self-contained entities." If this is not done, then the experience reveals itself as the "reality of both divine and human presence" (*AR*, 73). The experience of the divine-human movements is "not located in man's stream of consciousness--man understood in the immanentist sense--but in the In-Between of the divine and the human" (Ibid., 73). Consciousness' experienced movement toward divine reality *is* the constitution of consciousness itself. As Voegelin describes the matter elsewhere: "Existence in tension which is consciousness moves in two dimensions at the same time; it is eternal and mundanely timebound" (*Conversations*, 62). The form of existence we call consciousness is constituted by "the intersection of the time and the timeless" (Ibid.). The experience, properly understood, occurs somewhere between divine and human reality. The metaleptic story of Genesis 1 must therefore not be construed "hypostatically as a narrative told either by a revelatory God or by an intelligently imaginative human being" (*OH* V, 26). The story is both "because it is neither one nor the other" (Ibid.).

Through an analysis of the symbolism of Plato's *Timeaus*, Voegelin further examines these structures. The analysis must be considered because it serves both to point up a relation of equivalence between *Genesis* 1 and the *Timaeus* with regard to the symbolization of the It-reality and to indicate how the *Timaeus* offers us a further insight into the nature of the quest for the Beginning.

In the dialogue, Timaeus begins by duly invoking the help of the gods: "All men, Socrates, who have any degree of right feeling, at the beginning of every enterprise, whether small or great, always call upon God" (*Tim*, 27c). As he states, the invocation is all the more necessary given the nature of the inquiry: "And we, too, who are going to discourse of the nature of the universe, how created or how existing without creation, if we be not altogether out of our wits, must invoke the aid of the gods and goddesses and pray that our words may be above all acceptable to them and in consequence to ourselves" (Ibid.).

At the outset, the dialogue reveals the same quest for the Beginning that we discovered in Genesis 1. "Was the heaven ... or the world, whether called by this or by any other more appropriate name--assuming by name, I am asking a question which has to be asked at the beginning of an inquiry about anything--was the world, I say, always in existence and without beginning, or created, and had it a beginning" (*Tim*, 28b). Timaeus answers correctly: "Created, I reply, being visible and tangible and having a body, and therefore sensible, and all sensible things are apprehended by opinion and sense, and are in a process of creation and created" (Ibid.). However, all things that are created must have a cause, and this cause, given these remarks, quite obviously cannot be simply one more visible, tangible thing. Who, then, is the creator of heaven and the world, of the visible Cosmos? Voegelin summarizes Plato's answer: "The *aition* [the cause] of the Cosmos, its 'beginning,' is a paradigmatic order (*paradeigma*) designed by a divine Demiurge and, when found good by him by the standard of his own unenvious goodness, applied to the formation of the genetic Cosmos" (*OH* V, 90).

This Demiurge, this "Maker and Father" of the Cosmos who is "past finding out" (*Tim* 28c) is, however, not entirely free in his creative activity. Like the spirit of God in *Genesis* 1, who attempts to order an at least "passively resistant counterforce," Timaeus's Demiurge faces the necessary obstacle of Space when creating an ordered Cosmos. "The Demiurge is ... a something whose only relation to Space is his submission to the 'necessity' of creating 'things' when creatively devising at all" (*OH* V, 102). In our quest for the Beginning we arrive at the "penultimate mystery of a Cosmos that exists in the tension of Taxis-Ataxis, in the tension of thing-reality and It-reality," a mystery that "becomes luminous for the ultimate mystery of a Creator-God who, when he creates, has to create a tensional Cosmos" (Ibid., 103).

With this formulation, do we come to the End of our search for a Beginning? As Voegelin asks: Is the Demiurge "the Absolute in which the tensional questioning comes to its End?" (Ibid., 104). Voegelin answers: "The Demiurge is not an Absolute either" (Ibid.). The Demiurge cannot be the Beginning for which we are searching, because the act of creation is itself a tensional event. It is the tension between a "demiurgic will to create order and the 'necessary' obstacle of *chora* [space] that limits the creative will to thingness" (Ibid.).

If the analysis were to conclude at this stage, we would be left with a "dualism," a tensional conception of reality in suspense between two opposing forces. Consciousness' movement toward a reality or Beginning "beyond" the tensional Cosmos would be replaced by an ultimately tensional or dualistic reality from which there is no escape and in which there is no hope. The experienced longing of consciousness for the truth of reality beyond space and time would be brought to its conclusion through the symbolization of an absolute truth cognitively comprehended by consciousness in time.

According to Voegelin, Plato "avoids such a construction by symbolizing the poles of the tension themselves as tensional in nature" (*OH* V, 104). "Space at the lower pole of the complex is not a matter recognizable as such by its structure of a material element but a tensional something, symbolized metaphorically as a receptacle, or mother, or nurse of the visible Cosmos" (Ibid.). This tensional something, "because of its all receptiveness to the persuasion of noetic order is to be imagined as 'partaking' of noetic order (*tou noetou*) 'in an incomprehensible manner'" (Ibid.). At the upper pole, the Demiurge is also symbolized as tensional: "Does the noetic reality, symbolized as a 'Beyond' of the tension, not desire to go 'beyond' itself into the tension, just as the reality of Space, symbolized as a 'Beyond' of material thingness, is ready to go 'beyond' itself into thingly formed tensional reality?" (Ibid., 105). If, however, "the two poles of the mysterious tension each 'partake' in correlative tensionality of the reality of the other pole, would then the 'partaking' reality of the poles not be the one, true, mysterious reality rather than the tension symbolized by the poles?" (Ibid.).

In response, Voegelin writes that although Plato "appears to concede some sense to this possiblity ... any expectations of an ultimate symbolism will again be disappointed" (Ibid.). The "partaking" reality cannot be an ultimate symbolism, for it, too, would undermine consciousness' tensional experience of reality. The notion of "partaking," although resolving the problem of dualism, would do so only to negate the metaxic experience of consciousness. If reality were, in its eventually most considered sense, a partaking whole, the notion of "tension" would lose its sense. Consciousness would no longer experience itself in tension toward a reality beyond the tensional Cosmos for the simple reason that such a cosmos would not be tensional. There would be no Beyond of the tension, but only the partaking reality, a reality that simply *is*.

The test of both these symbolisms, the dualism of the Demiurge and Space and the non-tensional partaking reality, has been the concrete movements of consciousness. Neither were found satisfactory, for both failed to adequately reflect consciousness' quest for a Beginning beyond tensional reality, the Beginning of the It-reality, or, in Plato's language, the Cosmos. From this analysis Voegelin concludes that the mystery of the demiurgic god is, thus, not ultimate, but experienced as in tension toward the mystery of a divine reality that saves from the disorder of the Cosmos. The "*fides* of the Cosmos becomes transparent for a drama of the Beyond enacted, through the tensional process of the Cosmos, from a demiurgic Beginning to a salvational End" (*OH* V, 106). Consciousness experiences itself, not only as the product of a divine Beginning that moves creatively into the formation of a tensional cosmos, but also as a reality tending toward a divine End beyond the tensional Cosmos. Insofar as this divine End is experienced as beyond consciousness' understanding, so too will the divine Beginning be experienced as beyond consciousness understanding. The true beginning of reality cannot be understood until reality has come to its End: this End, however, always remains beyond man's understanding. The meaning of the tensional play of the cosmos of which man is a part is the ultimate mystery of existence, the mystery of "reality itself becoming luminous for its movement from the ineffable, through the Cosmos, to the ineffable" (Ibid., 103).

Does not this tension of the Beginning and the End lead us precisely to the form of dualism we have been attempting to avoid? Does it not suggest that reality is tensional through and through, that it exists in tension from a demiurgic god who creates an ordered Cosmos (a Cosmos that, due to the freedom of its members, tends toward a state of disorder), and a god who saves it from its disorder? Again, the test of the symbolism must be the movements of consciousness itself. In its quest for the truth of reality, consciousness experiences itself as in tension from its existence in thing-reality toward a reality beyond space and time, an eternal reality. The terms "Beginning" and "End," therefore, although burdened by the constraints of time, point not to two different divine realities, but to the oneness of a divine mystery beyond the tensional Cosmos. "The Beginning and the End of the story are experienced as a Beyond of the formative, tensional process of reality" (*OH* V, 106), that is, the tensional It-reality.[13]   This

---

[13]In our view, the divine Beyond is beyond the "formative, tensional process in reality," beyond the It-reality. However, Gerhart Niemeyer, in his essay "The Fulness of the Quest," seems to equate the tensional It-reality with "transcendence" and "divine reality." Gerhart Niemeyer, "The Fulness of the Quest" in *Eric Voegelin's Search for*

oneness of divine reality should not be understood as a monotheistic alternative to polytheism, however. The divine Beyond is not one God in competition with the many other gods, but the divine ground (*aition*) of the Cosmos. It is, as Voegelin asserts, "the tetragrammatic God beyond the personal God...beyond the God of dogmatic theology" (Ibid., 98). Voegelin has discussed the reality of this tetragrammatic God elsewhere. In his concluding reflections on time and history in *Order and History*, Volume IV, Voegelin states: "things do not happen in the astrophysical universe; the universe, together with all the things in it, happens in God" (*OH* IV, 334).

Consciousness, in its experience of movement toward a divine reality out of time, recognizes itself as part of a tensional reality, the meaning of which always remains beyond its understanding. The movement toward the truth of reality beyond space and time therefore has the paradoxic effect of revealing consciousness as being in a state of ignorance, of fundamental unknowing, with regard to the true meaning of its existence. As Voegelin writes:

> At the center of his existence man is unknown to himself and must remain so, for the part of being that calls itself man could be known fully only if the community of being and its drama in time were known as a whole. Man's partnership in being is the essence of his existence, and this essence depends on the whole, of which existence is a part. Knowledge of the whole, however, is precluded by the identity of the knower with the partner, and ignorance of the whole precludes essential knowledge of the part. This situation of ignorance with regard to the decisive core of

---

Order in History, S. A. McKnight, ed. (Baton Rouge: Louisiana State University Press, 1978), 211. There is indeed a textual basis for Niemeyer's interpretation. Voegelin asserts that the tension in the It-reality is "to be symbolized as divine." The difficulty with Niemeyer's analysis, however, is that it makes the "penultimate mystery of a Cosmos that exists...in the tension of thing-reality and It-reality" the "ultimate mystery" (*OH* V, 103). That is to say, it makes the "divine ordering force in the quest for truth" the "divine reality *beyond* the manifestation of its order in the event" (Ibid., 106). Such a construction would negate the experienced movement of consciousness toward a reality beyond tensional existence by making the tensional reality ultimate.

existence is more than disconcerting: it is profoundly disturbing, for from the depth of this ultimate ignorance wells up the anxiety of existence (*OH* I, 2).

In these pages we have spoken much about consciousness' quest for an order in existence beyond the disorder it experiences in its existence in space and time, a quest that becomes luminous for the movement of an It-reality from a divine Beginning to a salvational End. However, Voegelin's analysis will certainly invite question: Is the quest for the Beyond "real," or is it merely a misunderstood longing for some purely temporal reality that consciousness experiences as absent? Or is it a form of wishful thinking provoked by the seeker's inability to cope with the material circumstances of his life? In order to respond adequately to such questions, we must clarify the requisite structures of reality under whose conditions the quest can be made intelligible.

In his work *Anamnesis*, Voegelin discusses these same structures as they are manifested in Aristotle's *Metaphysics*. Through an analytic inversion of the movement of consciousness outlined by Aristotle, Voegelin clarifies the requisite structures in reality necessary for the advent of the quest: "Without the *kinesis* [movement] of being attracted by the ground, there would be no desire for it; without the desire, no questioning in confusion; without questioning in confusion, no awareness of ignorance" (*Anamnesis*, 149). That is, the human quest for the divine--in Aristotle's case, the directional movement of the *nous*--is predicated on the drawing power of the Beyond. Without this divine *kinesis*, the empirical fact of the quest would remain an underdetermined and, hence, inexplicable phenomenon of consciousness. Articulated in the language of our present analysis, if the formative force of the divine Beyond were not already present in the philosopher's quest for truth, the quest itself would be impossible.

If consciousness were to be conceived as a collection of immanent cognitive faculties, the symbols we have been describing under the aspect of luminosity would be inexplicable. Such inexplicability would not reflect a difficulty with the symbols themselves. Rather, it would reflect the fact that the experience of reality expressed by the symbols has become opaque. It would indicate that consciousness has lost contact with the experiences of reality that have engendered the luminous symbols. Moreover, once this "loss of contact" has become a pervasive existential phenomenon, the descriptive term "inexplicable" is soon replaced by the more radical term "meaningless." In the absence of the engendering experiences, the luminous symbols of consciousness simply cannot hold out.

The ensuing charge of meaninglessness is usually the result not of an argument but of a methodological prohibition of speech concerning dimensions of reality and experience deemed unacceptable by the adherents of a given "system" or philosophical school. As an example of this prohibition, Voegelin cites Marx's claim that the notion of "creation"--the idea that man is not the author of his own existence--is merely an "abstraction," an idea that makes "no sense," and this even though Marx concedes that it "is an idea that is rather deeply rooted in the consciousness of man" (*ER*, 290). The denial in these remarks is basic. It is not the result of a argument; rather, it is a refusal to apperceive the reality of human consciousness.

A subspecies of this general form of reductionism is the "psychology of projection." This view claims that the divine is merely a projection of consciousness, something ultimately human. It is in this regard that a thinker like Feuerbach can assert that "the divine being is nothing else than the human being."[14] "What was formerly contemplated and worshipped as God is now perceived to be something human."[15] "Man--this is the mystery of religion--projects his being into objectivity, and then again makes himself an object to this projected image of himself thus converted into a subject."[16] Given that God *is* merely a projection of man himself, Feuerbach indicates

---

[14]Ludwig Feuerbach, *The Essence of Christianity*, G. Eliot, trans. (New York: Prometheus Books, 1989), 14.

[15]Ibid., 13.

[16]Ibid., 29. Feuerbach goes on to say that although man makes himself an "object to God" through this act of projection, the act is ultimately in the interest of man himself: "In and through God, man has in view himself alone. It is true that man places the aim of his action in God, but God has no other aim of action than the moral and eternal salvation of man: thus man has in fact no other aim than himself. The divine activity is

the true task of humanity: "The spectre of God must be laid, and man must take back what he has thrown away by projecting it into a divine, supernatural existence" (*ER*, 280).

These various reductive analyses of luminous language and the reality it reveals hinge on a refusal to apperceive the phenomenon of the quest as it is constituted in the *metaxy* of the divine-human movements and countermovements. As Voegelin has argued, the quest, along with the symbols it engenders, is contingent on the drawing force of the divine presence in consciousness. It is not a movement that originates in a purely immanent human consciousness, but a loving response to the leading of the divine. Feuerbach's projectionist account of luminous language is therefore not merely false, but impossible, in that it retains the language as meaningful while denying its engendering source. It might be argued, however, that Feuerbach is guilty of no such thing because he interprets this language, not as luminous for divine reality, but as a "projection" of consciousness, that is, as something ultimately human. This suggestion, although having an appearance of credibility, is disingenuous, for whether or not the language is said to be a product of a purely immanent human consciousness, it obviously denotes something sufficiently non-human that it needs to be "taken back."

Although we have argued that the *kinesis* of the divine is essential for the advent of the quest, we have not yet shown how this can be discerned from an analysis of the quest itself. This will be the central thrust of what follows. Our analysis will take the form of the *via negativa*, arguing that a consciousness *unaided by the drawing of the divine Beyond* would be incapable of producing luminous symbols. We will argue for the truth of divine *kinesis*, not by direct demonstration, but by showing that a non-metaxic model of consciousness would be incapable of accounting for the symbolism of divine reality.

We can begin our analysis with the following question: How would temporal existence come to be understood as being in a state of disorder if there were not, already

---

not distinct from the human" (Ibid., 30).

in the heart of man, an apprehension of a true order beyond the disorder experienced? How could man recognize a deficiency in his existence in space and time in the absence of an apprehension of a reality of order in terms of which the deficiency could be determined?

The short answer to this question is that he could not, for the terms "disorder" and "deficiency" are relational in character; they are contingent for their meaning on the correlative terms to which they are opposed. Simply put, there can be no recognition of disorder in the absence of an apprehension of true order.[17] We should note that this contingency of meaning runs both ways. Not only is there no apprehension of disorder without an apprehension of order, there is also no apprehension of order without an apprehension of disorder. The two terms form a correlative set in which the meaning of both is determined. To remove them from this tensional set, that is, to use them as independently meaningful terms, results in nonsense.

Where does this lead us with regard to our present analysis? In what way does it help us resolve the question of the divine *kinesis*? Man clearly perceives his existence to be in a state of disorder. He apprehends, however limitedly or opaquely, a dimension of order beyond the disorder experienced.[18] However, how does consciousness,

---

[17]It is interesting to note here, for example, that even when a thinker claims that the whole of existence is absurd, that reality is deficient through and through, there is, implicit within his statement, the idea that there is at least one place or point at which reality is not absurd, i.e, his own consciousness. For the fact that one can recognize something as being absurd and, in turn, lament the fact that it is so, suggests that one is, on however limited a level, "other" than that which is absurd.

[18]The basis of this claim is the empirical fact that, on however low a level, man has historically claimed that existence in time does not measure up to the standards inherent in the longing of the human spirit, the longing for what is true, good, and beautiful. Regarding the concrete roots of this recognition of deficiency, Voegelin asserts: "At the basis of the experienced dissatisfaction lie the general miseries that afflict human existence, enumerated by Hesiod as hunger, hard work, disease, early death, and the injuries the weaker must suffer at the hands of the stronger" (*OH* V, 35).

unaided by the divine *kinesis*, attain such knowledge? From where in the experience of the objects and events in the spatio-temporal world is this understanding of order to be gained?

The answer here is precisely that it cannot be gained through this form of experience. The perception of the reality of disorder cannot by itself provoke a question concerning a dimension of order beyond the disorder experienced--an order not already present within consciousness--because in the absence of an apprehension of this order, the supposed disorder would not be perceived as such. The things perceived would simply be as they are and the descriptive term "disorder" would therefore have no sense. Furthermore, if the predicative term "disorder" has no meaning, the correlative language of divine order would be rendered just as meaningless. Stated differently, without the prior apprehension of order, the world of things would not become problematic for its existence, in other words, would not be understood as wanting of order. Reality would simply be as it *is*, thus preventing any question concerning *what it is not*--preventing, for example, a question concerning a divine realm of order beyond the temporal dimension of thingly reality. In light of these remarks it would appear that without the divine *kinesis*, consciousness could not "bootstrap" itself into a position where it could express symbolically its movement toward the Divine. The Divine must already be present in consciousness as a drawing force to which consciousness responds. In the absence of this divine movement, *there would be no quest*.

It is interesting to note that even modern ideologues acknowledge that the truth of reality is not exhausted by the structures of the spatio-temporal world.[19] They also

---

[19]Voegelin writes: "There should be stressed the frequently overlooked agreement of the deformers with the searchers for truth that reality is not exhausted by thingness in time. The resisters are just as conscious as the prophets and philosophers of the movement in reality beyond its present structure; and they know just as well that reality moves not only into a future of things but toward their Beyond. More recent symbolizations of deformative resistance, such as the 'transcendence into the future' (*Transzendenz in die Zukunft*), reveal by their very formulation the distinction they purpose to obscure; nor should be forgotten the contemporary enmity between certain representatives of 'positivism' and ideological activists" (*OH* V, 35).

attempt to transcend the disorder they experience in their personal and social lives, even if they do so by violently attempting to restructure reality according to their own image of existence. Although their "new" image is merely one more truncated, immanent conception of human existence--a conception equally susceptible to the charge of disorder as the one it replaces--it too reveals the transcending movements of consciousness as it responds to the divine calling. Even for the ideologue, the movement toward what is "beyond" is not in question. The difficulty, however, is that in the case of the ideologue, the *kinesis* of the divine Beyond is replaced by the dialectical movements of a purely immanent historical process. For the divine beyond is substituted the divine movements of "history" as it draws human existence along toward its immanent end. The ideologue, although obviously aware of the transcending movement in reality, draws the true *telos* of that movement into the immanent order of reality as the End of the quest to be brought about by revolutionary activity. History, it would appear, is unable to finish its course without the help of revolutionary thinkers such as Marx and Engels.

c) Reflective Distance

Thus far our analysis has involved an exploration of consciousness in its stuctural modes of intentionality and luminosity, and of reality in its corresponding dimensions of thing-reality and It-reality. This analysis, although explicitly concerned with these structures, also implicitly manifests the third dimension of consciousness, the "reflective distance" of consciousness to its own structure. Consciousness is structured, "not only by the paradox of intentionality and luminosity, but also by an awareness of the paradox, by a dimension to be characterized as a reflectively distancing remembrance" (*OH* V, 40). Through the course of our analysis, this mode of consciousness has been variously manifested through symbols such as "the tension of the metaxy," "the poles of the tension," "the things and their Beyond," "thing-reality and It-reality," "the human and the divine," "intentionality and luminosity" (Ibid.). Consciousness is aware of the nature of its participation in reality. As Voegelin asserts:

The thinker, it is true, cannot abolish the reflective distance of his consciousness to its own existential structure, but in his remembrance he can imaginatively forget this or that part of the paradoxically complex event; and when a thinker, whatever his motives may be, forgets his role as a partner in being, and with this role the metaleptic character of his quest, he can deform the remembered assertive power of imagination in his quest imaginatively into the sole power of truth (Ibid, 41).

The loss of reflective distance occurs when luminosity is eclipsed and consciousness is conceived as functioning solely in its mode of intentionality. Here, the structure of reflective distance comes to be understood, not as consciousness' "remembrance" of its place in the tensional process of reality, but as a sort of *transcendental reflection* from somewhere *outside* the process. From this Archimedean standpoint, both consciousness and the It-reality are conceived as "things," the relation between which must be determined by the transcendental consciousness presently engaged in the act of reflection. Questions concerning whether consciousness adequately reflects the structure of the It-reality, of whether the luminous symbols of consciousness constitute a correct representation of reality, then become the dominant philosophical problem. Depending on one's response to this dilemma, there arise the purely secondary philosophical phenomena of "scepticism," "realism," and "anti-realism." These phenomena are secondary because their articulation is contingent on a deformation of the primary metaxic structure of consciousness. Only when the luminous symbols of consciousness have been deformed into "concepts" denoting "things" can the transcendentalism from which these "positions" arise occur. The transcendentalism itself is a dubious act of *hubris*, an attempt to assume a god-like perspective *beyond* the experienced tension of consciousness that is limited by the true Beyond. While it is true that consciousness can indeed reflect on its symbolic movements in the *metaxy*, it cannot reflect on itself thus reflecting. The consciousness that reflects is the *same* consciousness that existentially participates in the process. To posit the existence of a second self which reflects on the structures of the first would result in either an infinite regression of reflective acts or a single reflective act whereby consciousness gains mastery over the process as a whole. Both of these positions deform the metaxic structure of consciousness.

Hegel's analysis of experience in his *Phenomenology* exhibits precisely the deformative structures presently under discussion. He wanted to replace the inconclusive "love of wisdom" with "wisdom possessed in the shape of absolute knowledge, by a conclusive *Wissenschaft* beyond the inconclusive love" (*OH* V, 50). In the concluding pages of the Introduction to the *Phenomenology*, Hegel asserts that what he is developing is a "Science of the Experience of Consciousness."[20]

There is nothing in this programmatic declaration that is unacceptable; however, it invites the question of what is meant by terms such as "science" and "experience." According to Hegel, consciousness' experience of reality is to be understood in the subject/object mode, on the level of intentionality. It is a consciousness of a "something." On the first level of experience, consciousness perceives its object as it is in itself, as it is "*per se*." When, through the process of experience, this object turns out to be different from what it was originally perceived to be, it becomes an object "for consciousness." Consciousness then appears to have two objects, the thing as it is *per se*, and as it is *per se* for consciousness. Hegel resolves this tension by asserting that through the dialectical movement of consciousness from the first object to the second, "the first object is altered; it ceases to be what it is *per se*, and becomes consciously something which is *per se* only *for consciousness*." "Consequently, then, what this real *per se* is for consciousness is truth; which, however, means that this is the essential reality, or the object which consciousness has."

As Hegel admits, the untruth of an object is usually indicated by "appealing to some other object which we may happen to find casually and externally."[21] This is

---

[20] G.W.F. Hegel, *Hegel: The Essential Writings*, F.G. Weiss, ed. (New York: Harper and Row, 1974), 53.

[21] Ibid., 52.

not the case with Hegel's dialectical movement, however. In his view, "the new object is seen to have come about by a *transformation* or *conversion* of consciousness itself," and "this way of looking at the matter is *our* doing, what *we* contribute."[22] In speaking of the initial impetus for consciousness' dissatisfaction with its knowledge on the first level of experience, a dissatisfaction that results in its movement toward true knowledge, Hegel claims that "consciousness suffers this violence at its own hands; it destroys its own limited satisfaction."[23]

As Voegelin asserts, the manifest structures of Hegel's analysis are recognizably the same as those of his own. They reveal "the paradox of intentionality-luminosity and the symbolic complex of consciousness-reality-language" (*OH* V, 56). Hegel, like Plato's prisoner in the Cave, is attempting to free himself from the shadows in the Cave, "be they doctrinal deformations of theology, propositional deformations of metaphysics or ontology, clever intellectualism, second-rate criticism or scepticism, etc." (Ibid.). In this sense, his analysis is sound. It is an act of resistance against the deformations prevalent in his time. The legitimate act of resistance soon becomes deformative, however; through the force of his resistance, Hegel arrogates God's role in the process to himself. As Voegelin asserts, "when we look for the light shining from the Beyond that forces (*anangkoito*), directly or through a mediator, the prisoner to turn, we receive instead the information that the *periagoge* is *unsere Zutat*, our addition or addendum" (Ibid.). It is no longer the Divine that leads consciousness toward itself, but consciousness that leads itself through its "self-assertive" action. Hegel's dialectic movement is not merely the existentially modest "quest" for divine truth, but a self-initiated process resulting in the resolution of consciousness' paradoxic structure in the form of "absolute knowledge." That is to say, Hegel's consciousness not only self-assertively moves toward the divine Beyond, but also becomes identical with it:

---

[22]Ibid.; emphasis mine.

[23]Ibid., 49.

In pressing forward to its true form of existence, consciousness will come to a point at which it lays aside its semblance of being hampered with what is foreign to it, with what is only for it and exists as an other; it will reach a position where appearance becomes identified with essence, where, in consequence, its exposition coincides with just this very point, this very stage of the science proper of mind. And, finally, when it grasps this its own essence, it will connote the nature of absolute knowledge itself.[24]

At this stage in the process, consciousness "is no longer compelled to go *beyond* itself," for it has "arrived at the point where it finds its own self, the point at which the concept corresponds to the object and the object to the concept."[25] Voegelin writes: The "*Geist* has come into its realm of truth," a truth which is apprehended by Hegel himself. Regarding its "presentation and content [Hegel] says: 'This realm is the truth, as it is without veil in and for itself. One can express oneself therefore in this manner: its content is the presentation of God as he is in his eternal being [*ewiges Wesen*] before the creation of nature and a finite *Geist*" (*OH* V, 62). Hegel imaginatively forgets the his place in the *metaxy*, in the In-Between of the divine-human movements and countermovements. The reflective distance of consciousness to its own structure is lost and, in turn, replaced by a "self-identical" consciousness which assumes a vantage point *beyond* tensional reality.

Regardless of Hegel's declaration that history has been brought to its End through his "system of science," history itself seems reluctant to comply. People continue to engage in the modest task of "philosophy," the loving quest for the Divine; they continue to produce luminous symbols that reflect the structure of that quest; and they do so realizing they will never bring the search to its end. Man recognizes from the quest itself that there is no place "beyond" or "outside" the tension; tensional existence is the lot of man in reality, the lot with which he must cope in the ordering of his life. The lot of man in reality is not experienced as absurd as long as the poles of the tension are not

---

[24]Ibid., 54.

[25]Ibid., 48.

hypostatized and one does not attempt to draw the Beyond into the immanent order of temporal existence. Existence becomes absurd only when one imagines oneself capable of incarnating the Divine in the spatio-temporal world. The attempt makes reality senseless, for reality continually fails to actualize the promised kingdom in the immanent realm, and, hence, one finds oneself in the existentially disturbing position of awaiting, or violently stuggling for, a realm of order that never comes.

CHAPTER TWO

_____

DIFFERENCES, DOGMAS, AND DEFORMATIONS

To briefly summarize the findings of our previous discussion, we must say that a true theology, if it is to be true at all, must be guided, and hence limited, by the structures of consciousness as they are reflectively present to consciousness itself. A true theology is one that pays close attention to the nature of reality. The reason such a remark is necessary is that, in modern discourse, we are constantly bombarded by the fantastic dreams of those who, being dissatisfied with these structures--dissatisfied with the nature of reality itself, seek to abolish that reality by liberating us from both ourselves and the transcendent. It is important to keep in mind that in this century the greatest crimes against the spirit have been committed precisely in the name of the Spirit.

In opposition to such visions, our findings have been considerably more modest. In our search for the Divine we have found, not a formula whereby man through a cognitive or political act can bootstrap himself into the place of God, but the fact that human existence is always limited by the horizon of mystery. Man, although he recognizes in his consciousness a longing for a truth or dimension of reality and space, is always limited by the fact of his finitude. The process or movement of consciousness is never realized, in terms of its End, in the immanent order of things.

Furthermore, we found that consciousness, due to both its own manifold structure and the manifold structure of reality, employs several different symbolic forms in order to articulate its experience of reality. Luminous symbols are those that express consciousness' participation in the It-reality, while intentional linguistic the symbols are employed by consciousness to denote objects and events in the external world. Moreover, the confusion of these two forms of symbolization lies at the heart of much of the erroneous theological work done in modernity. Many theologians and philosophers, having accepted intentionality as the only legitimate mode of discourse, have engaged in the futile endeavour of trying to find a form of religious discourse that accommodates the methodological restriction, while simultaneously attempting to retain the meaning of symbols such as "God," "divine," and "transcendent."[26] The task, as history now reveals, was doomed to fail. Once the methodological restriction is accepted, the language symbols cannot holdout, and once the language symbols have been rendered meaningless, the reality they express will soon be obscured.

The third structure of consciousness discussed was reflective distance. Consciousness is characterized not only by certain structures, but by a reflective awareness of those structures. Through a reflective analysis of the symbols employed by consciousness, one can become aware of the tensional structure of human existence in the *metaxy*. If these structures are forgotten, however, if one imaginatively forgets one's place in reality, then theological deformations of the type mentioned above, along with a host of others, become possible.

With regard to the content of the present chapter, our task will be to outline and critically assess three of these deformative conceptions of consciousness, three false theologies. All reflect, more or less explicitly, a forgetfulness of reality. The deformer is one who, failing to apperceive or even refusing to apperceive the nature of his own

---

[26]Consider the debate between Antony Flew, Basil Mitchell, R.M. Hare and I.M. Crombie on the question of falsification "Theology and Falsification," *Philosophy of Religion*, W.I. Rowe, W.J. Wainwright, eds. (New York: Harcourt Brace Jovanovich, 1973), 419-428. As an example of the "deconstructionist" response to this sort of theological linguistic analysis, see Mark C. Taylor, *Erring: A Postmodern A/theology* (Chicago: The University of Chicago Press, 1984).

existence, chooses to live in what Voegelin, following Musil, has described as a "second reality"--a world of one's imagination as opposed to the reality of one's existence.

The first deformation to be discussed is that of subjectivism and symbolic difference. Here we will outline in more detail than was presented in Chapter One the contours of the position, paying particular attention to the problem of hypostatization as it pertains to the search for a constant in human experience. The central difficulty with this position is the radical privatization of experience, both religious and otherwise. Once this view is accepted, truth and reality become matters of individual preference. The problem, is, however, that once experience is thus understood, the possibility of genuine dialogue and, in turn, the rational resolution of competing interests become well-nigh impossible. In this sense, the view has far-reaching political consequences.

The second phenomenon to be dealt with is that of dogma and the loss of meaning. As this title suggests, in such a view the meaning of language is lost, not through an outright prohibition, but through its separation from experience. Of particular importance here is the notion of change of meaning. Once language has been separated from existence, meaning becomes little more than a matter of semantics. We will discuss as a matrix of our analysis, the changes of meaning that the symbols "God" and "man" undergo in Feuerbach's theory of projection.

The final matter to be considered in this chapter is what Voegelin has described as the "prohibition of the Question." Here we will examine, in the work of both Richard Rorty and Karl Marx, the outright refusal to permit the act of questioning. In Marx's case, the prohibition is overt: man simply should not ask questions concerning the meaning of his life which move beyond the parameters stipulated by Marx's conception of consciousness and history. In Rorty's case, the refusal to question is more subtle. One is, permitted to ask such questions, at least ostensibly. This apparent openness is undermined, however, by the fact that in Rorty's view, all linguistic forms are merely by-products of the contingency of human speech and action. One can speak about whatever one pleases, provided, of course, that one's speech is not thought to reflect anything, not thought to say something true about reality. If one insists on speaking in *this* way, questioning and conversation will necessarily have to come to an end.

1. Subjectivism and Symbolic Difference

Let us begin by restating several of the questions that arose in response to our earlier discussion of symbolization, experience, and the problem of universality: What is meant by the term "equivalences," given that the symbols that constitute the historical field appear, at least on the surface, to be quite different and perhaps even "incommensurable"? How is one form of symbolization determined to be "superior" to another while simultaneously said to be equivalent? What is the constant structure of the reality of consciousness that constitutes the criterion by which certain symbols are understood as deformative?

The latter question raises the problem of universality in Voegelin's work. Voegelin does not consider his understanding of consciousness to be merely his own personal preference. He is not a subjectivist, relativist, or historicist and, hence, does not maintain that symbolic forms are legitimated on the basis of individuated private experience. Rather, Voegelin claims that notions such as "existential tension," "the *metaxy*," and "tension toward the divine" are descriptive of structures of consciousness that hold universally, that is, in the case of "all men."

> There is more than one symbolic form, because the experience of reality varies in the dimension of compactness and differentiation, *as well as of deformations through contraction of existence and fallacious hypostases.* These various modes of experience require different symbols for their adequate expression, *while the reality experienced and symbolized remains recognizably the same.* In dealing with this issue, Aristotle discovered the relation of equivalence between symbolic forms. Two symbolisms are equivalent in spite of their phenotypical differences, if they refer recognizably to the same structures in reality (*OH* IV, 188; emphasis mine).

From these remarks it seems obvious enough that the universality we are seeking is to be found neither in the symbols nor in the experience, for different symbolic forms are produced by different types of experience. However, if the difference extends as far as the engendering experience, one wonders where universality or equivalence is to be found. The short answer to this question is: In the reality in which consciousness exists. What is constant in reality is the structure of reality itself, a structure that even deformations cannot negate.

This answer may not be acceptable to someone who prefers a contracted existence. The deformer might insist that both his experience of reality and the symbolic articulation of that experience are different from that of the person in existential tension and that hence there is nothing left in consciousness by which his experience and symbolization could be judged to be deformative. He could claim that in the absence of some criterion inherent to his own consciousness, the notions of deformation and universality are senseless. It must be stated that the deformer would be right in his assertion that there is no thing by which his deformation could be determined as such, and yet he would be wrong in his conclusion that the notion of deformation itself is therefore senseless. The intelligibility of the deformer's sceptical challenge rests on a methodological restriction concerning the type of answer he will accept. Although he admits that "no thing" can be found to justify the language of universality and deformation, nonetheless, he claims that such a "thing" *must be found* if the dilemma is to be resolved. The appropriate response to such an argument is not to begin casting about in search of the object in question, for to do so would be to accept the conditions of a challenge that cannot be answered on its own terms. Rather, we must point up the place at which the initial deformation occurs. Our response, therefore, is that consciousness is *not a thing*, it is not a something that can be deformed in the same way that any object in the spatio-temporal world can be deformed. As Voegelin asserts, "there is no erotic tension lying around somewhere" waiting to be "investigated," "expressed," or "deformed" (*OH* V, 186). Rather, the metaxic structure of consciousness indicates a way of participating in reality, i.e., the appropriate manner of comporting oneself in relation to the various levels of being.

To better understand consciousness' participation in the order of being, consider the phenomenon of love. We all understand love to be part of our experience of reality. However, love is not a thing that one can circumscribe as an object to be investigated. Rather, it is a dimension of experience that manifests itself in the movements of consciousness. We know that one can love and that one can refuse to do so; further, we know that when the latter option carries the day, something in man's experience of reality has been lost or deformed. But what has been lost is not a thing. Furthermore, when we say that human beings become less or other than what they are in reality through a refusal to love, we are not saying that there is a thing called love lying around in consciousness that serves as the criterion by which terms like "less" and "other" have their meaning. There is no such "thing." However, in spite of the rather curious nature of this phenomenon, we do indeed claim to recognize a deficiency in existence when human beings refuse to love.

To return to our discussion of consciousness, let us indicate briefly how the misunderstanding that underlies the questions with which we began our discussion occurs. The attempt to get outside human consciousness in order to reflect on it as an object is necessarily an attempt to get outside the tension toward the divine, because human consciousness is not a immanent thing, but is structurally constituted by the presence of divine reality. In light of this structure, then, Voegelin asserts:

> The term *consciousness*, therefore, could no longer mean to me a human consciousness that is conscious of a reality outside of man's consciousness, but had to mean the In-Between reality of the participatory pure experience that then analytically can be characterized through such terms as the poles of the experiential tension, and the reality of the experiential tension in the *metaxy* (*AR*, 73).

In order for consciousness to be conceived as a thing--an object of a transcendental subject--it would have to be capable of transcending, not only its own structure, but also the divine pole of the experiential tension. Man would have to become a god. However, because man cannot cease to be man, such forms of transcendental reflection must be understood as hubristic acts that result, not merely in misguided philosophical squabbles, but in a deformation of our understanding of reality.

Consciousness *is* precisely as it presents itself in its symbolic articulation of its experience of reality. There is nothing more than this, no "additional experience of man's nature" by which one could adjudicate on the veridical or fallacious, formative or deformative, nature of a given symbolic form (*EESH*, 234). "Truth," according to Voegelin, "has its reality in the symbols engendered by the quest, and the quest has its reality in the metaxy of divine-human movements and countermovements. The symbols, thus, arise from the human response to the appeal of reality, and the response is burdened with its character as an event in the reality to which it responds" (*OH* V, 37).

Voegelin's analysis answers the advocates of subjectivism adequately. But does it fall prey to a different sort of subjectivism--one that affirms the legitimacy of private opinion on the grounds that there exists no commonly held standard of rationality whereby one can adjudicate between competing conceptions of reality? James Wiser expresses such concerns about Voegelin's analysis in his essay "Philosophy as Inquiry and Persuasion."[27] He argues that insofar as the "truth of metaleptic existence is not self-evident," and insofar as philosophy, if it "is to perform its public function...must be able to justify its claim to public attention," Voegelin must say more in order to legitimate the conception of consciousness and reality he espouses.[28] According to Wiser, the three areas in which this might be done are as follows:

---

[27]Wiser is not the only one to have expressed such concerns. See also John Hallowell, "Existence in Tension" in *Eric Voegelin's Search for Order in History Search for Order in History*,S. A. McKnight, ed. (Baton Rouge: Louisiana State University Press, (1978), 125-26.

[28]James L. Wiser, "Philosophy as Inquiry and Persuasion" in *Eric Voegelin's Search for Order in History*, S.A. McKnight, ed. (Baton Rouge: Louisiana State University Press, 1978), 138.

1) Voegelin believes there is a fundamental reality or an ontological ground according to which the adequacy of opinions can be measured. Consequently his personalism does not necessarily imply a subjectivism.

2) Voegelin speaks of a set of primary experiences available to all men, which form the basis for any attempt at symbolic representation. Thus his mysticism is not necessarily a relativism.

3) Voegelin appears to believe in a constant revealed by its intention to participate in the In-Between of human existence. Thus the form of open existence is not simply the private preference of a single individual.[29]

For Wiser, the engendering source of the concern expressed by these remarks is Voegelin's refusal to make a hard distinction between reason and faith, a refusal which seems to put the possibility of rational persuasion on rather tenuous ground.[30] This is not to suggest that Wiser finds Voegelin's position untenable. His request is merely that Voegelin address the problem directly. He even goes so far as to indicate where such an analysis might begin; nevertheless, one suspects that Wiser's concern is that once the distinction between reason and faith has been eliminated, faith emerges the victor and reason is allocated to a merely subsidiary role.

There is a textual basis for Wiser's concern. There are many instances throughout Voegelin's work where, when such questions present themselves, one instead receives the counsel that the validity of the analysis rests on man's "trust" or "faith" in the order of reality. To mention but a few:

The most intimate truth of reality, the truth about the meaning of the cosmic play in which man must act his role with his life as the stake, is a mythopoetic play linking the psyche of man in trust with the depth of the Cosmos (*EESH*, 229).

The imaginative play has its hard core of reality as it is motivated by man's trust (*pistis*) in reality as intelligibly ordered, as a Cosmos (Ibid., 228).

---

[29]Ibid., 138.

[30]Ibid.

The trust in the Cosmos and its depth is the source of the premises--be it the generality of human nature or, in our case, the reality of the process as a moving presence--that we accept as the context of meaning for our concrete engagement in the search of truth (Ibid., 234).

What is true in these remarks is that, on its deepest level, our understanding of reality is not substantiated by means of a "proof" in its sense as "demonstration." Logical demonstration does not get us far, because the validity of a given proof is always contingent on one's primary existential commitments, and such existential commitments cannot be derived from the purely formal categories of logical analysis. This is not to say that these commitments cannot be supported with reason. Reason indeed plays a role in validating one's experience of reality. However, reason must not be understood in the truncated sense so prevalent in modernity. Rather, following the classical thinkers, reason is an "openness toward reality" that manifests itself in a willingness to apperceive the structure of existence as it becomes luminous in human consciousness. Admittedly, this understanding of reason cannot remove all doubt; however, this does not imply a deficiency. Rather, it points up the fact that the expectation of certitude is misplaced with regard to questions concerning the meaning of existence.

In light of these remarks, then, we must say that Wiser's concern is misplaced if the reasons he seeks are of the demonstrative sort mentioned above. Such reasons are not possible. However, if the reasons he desires are of the classical type we have just discussed, then an adequate form of justification can indeed be found in Voegelin's analysis--one that removes the threat of subjectivism while avoiding the equally undesirable notion of absolute knowledge.

To return to our discussion of subjectivism, we can analytically distinguish two difficulties the position raises: the problem of incommensurability and question of intersubjective communication. The former problem is the question of how human experience is constituted, whether by individuated subjective factors or by those that are common to all men. The latter question addresses the same issue from a different perspective. It begins with the fact that human beings are able to communicate with one another and then asks what is the nature of human experience that makes this communication possible. The question we will discuss first is whether or not a subjectivist conception of reality, experience, and language-- the notion that all men are *not the same* in that their experience of reality is significantly different--can actually be made intelligible and hence have any philosophical force. Voegelin's response is unequivocal: he says no! This response is not stated explicitly, but takes the form of a positive affirmation of the proposition's contrary: "We all know that all men are men even if we don't know what man is, or what differentiated consciousness is, or anything like that" (*Conversations*, 56). For Voegelin, the "background of the general element is the fact that behind all revelatory language, behind all philosophical language, behind all noetic theology or any other theology, there lies, of course, the common experience of all men in the cosmos in which they live" (Ibid.). This is also what makes Aristotle's claim that "all men by nature desire to know" universally legitimate. Beyond these positive remarks, Voegelin clarifies his argument by stating it negatively. He states that without this primary experience "we wouldn't know what a philosopher or theologian means when he talks about God" (Ibid., 57). The possibility of understanding--an understanding which, empirically, we know to be real--is predicated on a commonality of experience.

On the basis of these statements we can articulate the general contours of Voegelin's argument against subjectivism. As we have said, the claims that all men are not the same and that human experience is not universal are essential to the subjectivist position. However, the assertion that all men experience the world differently is intelligible only under the assumption of commensurability. The affirmation of difference can be made intelligible only if there exist commonly accepted standards by which any difference might be determined. Determinant difference implies commensurability. Yet, it is precisely this commensurability that is lacking in the conception of subjectivism outlined above.

The difficulty with the position can be articulated as follows: the subjectivist who affirms the general statement "all men experience reality differently" must, in order for us to understand him, indicate precisely what the difference is. However, this is precisely what he cannot tell us, because he is prohibited from understanding and expressing this by the position itself. The notion of difference, therefore, becomes unintelligible, and, along with it, the very idea of subjectivism.

Voegelin's account of the "cosmic primary experience" is his strongest refutation of subjectivism. The primary experience is the "pre-philosophical, pre-theological, pre-revelatory" understanding of reality that makes the fact of our language and communication intelligible. Concerning the nature of this experience, Voegelin asserts that it is a "knowledge of the cosmos with all of its contents--gods, men, the world and so on" (*Conversations*, 56). The inclusion of an understanding of the gods within the experience indicates that if divine reality were not a part of the primary experience of the Cosmos, we would be unable to understand any religious symbolization, even the religious symbolization of a philosopher. The experience must be there; if it were not, the symbols simply would not arise.[31]

Our subjectivist might wish to take exception to this formulation. He might insist that although a significant level of commonality of experience is essential for communication, an apprehension of divine reality is not included within that experience. Admittedly, this is a greatly attenuated form of subjectivism, yet it is nonetheless one that has become pervasive in modernity. In order to maintain such a view, some account must be given of symbolic utterances that point to a divine dimension in reality, an account that renders them inapplicable to the experience of others. One of the most commonly employed methods is to argue that the symbols have no sense, that they are meaningless. However, such a claim is disingenuous. The one who makes it clearly knows what the symbols mean; if he did not, the negation itself would make no sense.

---

[31]Jurgen Gebhardt states the matter similarly: "Partnership in being, as revealed in man's quest for his humanity, is the precondition of the possibility of language *per se*" (Jurgen Gebhardt, "Epilogue," *OH* V, 118).

Where have we arrived as a result of this analysis? Let us briefly list our discoveries: We have found that consciousness is not a thing; and that the deformation of one's experience and symbolic utterances is not the misplacing or distorting of a something, but the hiding or ignoring or covering over of the non-thingly structure of consciousness. We have also found that the universal in consciousness is the "primary experience of the cosmos," an experience which includes all of the various realms of being and the divine ground of reality. Finally, we have found that a refutation of subjectivism, in both its radical and modified forms, can be developed through an appeal to the primary experience.

2. Dogma and the Loss of Meaning

As we have already indicated, true understanding is not primarily a matter of semantics, but of existence. In order to apprehend the truth of reality, one must orient one's soul toward it; one must live in it, participate in it. To fail to do so results not simply in a "falsehood in words," but in a more profound falsehood, an "essential" or "unmixed" falsehood in the soul, of which the verbal falsehood is merely a "copy" or "after-rising image" (*Rep*, 382b). This primacy of existence over language affords us a further insight into the nature of symbolization and its deformation.

The meaning of a given linguistic symbol is determined by the nature of the experience that it was originally intended to express. The meaning is already there; it sets the parameters for meaningful speech and the standards by which deformative interpretations are to be judged. In modern philosophical discourse, however, there predominates the view that language can be made to mean anything at all, that meanings can be changed at will to suit the purposes of a given speaker. What are the conditions upon which a change of meaning is predicated? How are we to distinguish between justified changes and those that are suspect?

First, it must be stated that the notion "change of meaning" has sense only under the assumption that one understands the symbol's original meaning. Once this is understood, certain misguided forms of argumentation, for example, arguments from meaninglessness, are revealed as having a circular structure in that they are predicated on the meaningful use of precisely the term they claim is meaningless. Furthermore, arguments that separate language and reality experienced are revealed to alter the very notion of meaning.

On the most basic level, such arguments claim that symbols *mean* what they mean solely on the basis of what *we say they mean*. Meaning is understood as non-relational in character. Those who endorse semantic arguments of this type must make their case on the basis of the symbols themselves, for, by their own admission, meaning pertains to nothing beyond the realm of language. The idea that symbols have their meaning through their expression of one's experience of reality is simply thrown out.

Such an argument undermines itself, however. Once language has been cut loose from reality, no argument is possible; rather, all that remains, as Voegelin puts it, is the question: "Who pulls the gun first?" (*Conversations*, 69). Hence, in order to argue that a word does not "mean" this or that, it is necessary to argue about something other than the word itself. Conversely, if the word is taken on its own, in abstraction from existence, one wonders from where exactly the discontent arises. How could the word "God," for example, be said *not to mean* "the divine reality beyond time," if meaning were simply a matter of syntax? On what basis is the original meaning determined to be deficient? The only response possible is something like "Because *I* say it's deficient!" However, this gets us no further; the assertion adds nothing to understanding, because the simple statement of preference does not offers us a criterion, the content of which would make the charge of deficiency intelligible. This is because the statement taken on its own is *empty of content*. What is lost through this form of argumentation is not merely the meaning of a particular symbol, but the notion of meaning *per se*.

This abuse of language, euphemistically described as a "change of meaning," has certain Orwellian overtones. When one reads in Feuerbach, for example, that "the absolute being, the God of man, *is* the being of man itself," one is reminded of "doublethink," the central tenet of "newspeak," that permitted its users both to "believe" and to "know" that contraries can be meaningfully affirmed in the same breath, even the same word. The similarity between Orwell's doublethink and the version of it prevalent in modernity can be found in Feuerbach's affirmation of a relation of equivalence between the symbols "God" and "man." As Feuerbach writes, "God is the nature of man regarded as absolute truth,--the truth of man."[32] To the common observer, however, the statement "Man *is* God" seems to involve a rather fundamental misunderstanding of the symbols. As we have argued, language does not stand on its own but receives its meaning through its expression of human experience. Once removed from that experience, words lose their sense or are emptied of content, and when the parameters that delineate meaningful speech are absent, almost any concatenation of symbols appears possible. Language, then, becomes an infidel; it is faithful to nothing, not even itself.

Once brought to light, this deformation not only reveals its own structure, but also points the way to meaningful discourse. Broadly stated, our task here is to return to the reality from which the symbols have emerged. As Voegelin states regarding his own endeavours: "The methodologically first, and perhaps the most important, rule of my work is to go back to the experiences that engender symbols" (*AR*, 97). A proposition such as Feuerbach's, then, must be tested, not in the abstract, but in the context from which the symbols originally emerged.

When we put the statement "Man *is* God" in the mouth of a real human being, we find that its plausibility becomes rather tenuous. Two interpretations are possible: If we take the statement to mean that our language concerning the divine is now to be understood as descriptive of man, the difficulty we encounter is that concrete human existence is limited by the phenomenon of death. Death has always been one of the more uncomfortable anomalies for those prone to self-deification, for, even though one *can say* that "Man *is* God," one must ultimately reckon with the structure of human existence itself, and death hardly seems the appropriate end for a deity. In fact, the symbol "God"

---

[32]Feuerbach, *The Essence of Christianity*, 19.

refers to a dimension of reality *beyond* the immanent realm and hence *beyond* death. Man, then, cannot be a god--he cannot, but not because he cannot say it; rather, it is because his existence will not permit it. Reality does not allow him to live like a god. Might we have misunderstood Feuerbach? Is it possible that what is meant by the proposition is not that man is like God, but rather, that God is like man? Is the symbol "God" one that we normally take to characterize human existence? With this interpretation of Feuerbach, a different problem arises. If the symbol "God" means, in its eventually most considered sense, "man," one wonders what the purpose of the redefinition is. That is, if the symbol "man" is perfectly in order, then the addition of the symbol "God" would appear to be redundant. The charge of redundancy, however, is too charitable; it does not make clear the truly deformative character of the proposition.

As we have argued, the proposition "Man *is* God" adds nothing to the meaning of the symbol "man." What, then, is the need for the proposition? The reason is this: the symbol "God," although appearing to have undergone a change of meaning, is, in fact, used in its original sense. If this were not the case, the position would become *uninteresting*. One would hardly get an audience if one where simply to say "man *is* man." The proposition relies for its appeal on a dubious semantic game: it must appear to change the meanings of the symbols in order to present itself as a new insight; however, it must do so while simultaneously retaining the old meanings, for without them it would reveal itself as an empty tautology.

There is a futher problem of dogma that remains to be considered. The issue pertains to the question of the distinction between the written word and the spoken word. Our discussion will centre around Plato's analysis of the matter in the *Phaedrus*. The text is particularly appropriate given the resurgence of interest in the question in modern philosophical discourse.[33]

---

[33]For an interesting discussion of this matter, see Charles Griswold, *Self-Knowledge in Plato's Phaedrus* (New Haven: Yale University Press, 1986), 202-229. For a very different treatment of the subject, see Jacques Derrida's "Pharmacia" in his *Dissemination*, B. Johnson, trans. (Chicago: The University of Chicago Press, 1981), 65-171.

In the *Phaedrus*, Plato has Socrates recount an Egyptian tale wherein an old god, Theuth, comes to the king of the region, Thamus, in order to present the various arts he has invented. Among these is the art of writing, which, according to Theuth, "provides a recipe for memory and wisdom" (*Phaedrus*, 274c). Thamus, however, begs to differ on both counts. He states that "if men learn this, it will implant forgetfulness in their souls; they will cease to exercise memory because they rely on that which is written" (275a). Furthermore, he tells Theuth that "it is no true wisdom that you offer your disciples, but only a semblance, for by telling them many things without teaching them you will make them seem to know much, while for the most part they know nothing" (275a-b). In the dialogue, Socrates sides with Thamus and asks Phaedrus if he knows of "another sort of discourse;" he seeks the sort of discourse that is "brother to the written speech," but which is of unquestioned legitimacy ... the sort that goes together with knowledge, and is written in the soul of the learner, that can defend itself, and knows to whom it should speak and to whom it should say nothing" (276a). Phaedrus gives the correct reply: "You mean no dead discourse, but the living speech, the original of which the written discourse may fairly be called a kind of image" (276a).

Living speech "goes together with knowledge," while written speech is merely an image or copy of living speech and provides only a "semblance" of knowledge. Language, once it assumes the form of an "external mark," is removed from the real in the same way that a painting, although it may be a copy of real things, is not itself *real* in the same sense as the objects it portrays (275d).

These remarks point up an insight that can also be found in Voegelin's work. Written words, according to Plato, constitute a "dead discourse," for although "they seem to talk to you as though they were intelligent ... if you ask them anything about what they say ... they go on telling you the same thing forever" (275d). Similarly, Voegelin considers dogmatic statements, that is, doctrinal propositions concerning the truth of reality, to be "static" or "dead," in part because they make dialogue impossible.

According to Voegelin, this is the reason why ideologues make such poor discussants. In a genuine dialogue they have nothing to say, because, beyond the mere repetition of their position, there is nothing more to be said. From the perspective of the dogmatic possessor of wisdom, the truth to which all dialogical endeavours are directed has been attained; consequently, questioning--the dialogical manifestation of the open soul--becomes a senseless activity. The dialogic pursuit of wisdom is thus replaced by wisdom possessed in the form of propositions denoting an exhaustive truth of reality. Granted, Voegelin does not assert that this difficulty arises merely from the fact that the words are written down; however, this does not render the comparison untenable. The similarity is not to be found between the phenomena themselves, that is, between the written word and the ideologue's recalcitrance, but rather in the implications that both have for the pursuit of reality.

In the *Protagoras* Plato describes the Sophists, with respect to the way they comport themselves in conversation, as those who "go on ringing in a long harangue, like brazen vessels, which when struck continue to sound" (*Prot.*, 329a). Interestingly, this description bears striking similarity to the account of the written word in the *Phaedrus*: "They [written words] seem to talk to you as though they were intelligent, but if you ask them anything about what they say ... they go on telling you just the same thing forever" (*Phaedrus*, 275d). The Sophist, with his rhetorical speechmaking, is, like the written word, incorrigible; he refuses to enter into dialogue, for to do so would be to expose himself to questions--questions which would certainly test the legitimacy of his views.

3. The Prohibition of the Question

Man, in his existence *in time*, is aware of a movement in his consciousness toward a truth of reality *beyond time*. He is aware that the truth of existence is not exhausted by the events and objects that constitute the spatio-temporal world. When man's consciousness becomes sufficiently differentiated, this structural movement toward the divine can be articulated in the form of a question--the Question concerning the meaning of existence.

The Question is not incidental to human behaviour, but is an essential dimension of man's participation in reality. As Voegelin states, "the Question capitalized is not a question concerning the nature of this or that object in the external world, but a structure inherent to the experience of reality" (*OH* IV, 317). In terms of its directional movement, the Question pushes beyond all existing things to their divine ground, a ground that can never be comprehended by consciousness, even though it is present in the questioning movements of consciousness. The possibility of a complete answer to the Question is precluded. However, the impossibility of a complete answer is insufficient reason to deny the Question. The ideologue's reluctance to engage in dialogue is just such a denial. His refusal to acknowledge the fact of the Question and his insistence on the truth of his propositions reveals that he is motivated by a desire to deny the mystery of reality "that has no end in time" (Ibid., 333).

Doderer has called this phenomenon the "refusal to apperceive." It has become all too familiar in modern philosophical discourse. Philosophy as a comprehensive system, whether it be Marx's immanentist historical materialism, Hegel's conclusive System of Science, or the relativistic absolutism of modern liberalism, has become so much the dominant mode of thinking about reality that true dialogic exchanges have become well-nigh impossible. For example, Marx understands religion as nothing but "imaginary flowers" that decorate the chains unjustly binding human existence (*ER*, 280). Once these chains have been broken, man will be able to regain his reason and "move around himself as around his real sun" (Ibid.). When the "'beyond of truth' has disappeared, it will be 'the task of history' to establish 'the truth of this world'" (Ibid.). And the truth of this world is that "Man is the world of man" (Ibid.). In this way, the mystery of the cosmos is abolished, and, along with it, the Question. Man no longer need search beyond himself, for the truth that has evaded him has done so, not by distance, but by proximity.

According to Marx, man lives in a state of alienation so long as he owes his existence to somebody or something else. The liberation of man and the establishment of a perfect realm of freedom, therefore, requires the "overthrow of all relationships in which man is a humiliated, oppressed, neglected, despised being" (*ER*, 279). Liberation in the socio-economic sphere requires the control of the means of production.

But the revolutionary transformation of man requires something more fundamental--the liberation from God. As Marx states, "the critique of religion is the presupposition of all critique" (Ibid.). The necessity of liberation from God derives from Marx's conception of the "total" or "socialistic man," the man who has completely regained himself from alienated existence. A human being of this type is "independent ... only when it stands on its own feet; and it stands on its own feet only when it owes its existence to nobody but itself" (Ibid., 289). Conversely, "a man who lives by the grace of somebody else is dependent"; and, as Voegelin says about his own existence, "I live most completely by the grace of somebody else when he 'has created my life,' when the source of my life lies outside myself" (Ibid., 289-90).

There is hardly a more profound sense in which a being can be dependent than by owing its very existence to the creative will of another. Even Marx sadly concedes that the idea of creation "is rather deeply rooted in the consciousness of man" (Ibid., 290). Nonetheless, Marx holds to his position and draws the conclusion that the questions through which the awareness of transcendence lives must not be permitted. In answer to anyone who asks: "From whence does my being come?"; "Why is there something, why not nothing?"; "What is the ground of my existence which, although not comprehended by my consciousness, is nonetheless present within it as a drawing force?" Marx's response is unequivocal: "Don't ask such questions; they are 'abstractions'; they make 'no sense'; stick to the reality of being and becoming" (Ibid., 290). With Marx, no conversation about religion is possible.

The prohibition of questioning is not confined to Marx and Marxists. It can be found in slightly different symbolic apparel in contemporary philosophical writings.

Take, for example, the work of Richard Rorty. In *Contingency, Irony, and Solidarity*, he argues that "intellectual and moral progress" is not a matter of increasing our "understanding of the way things are," but of increasing the "usefulness" of certain "metaphors."[34] The task of philosophy, therefore, is not to seek out the truth of reality, but to attempt to "redescribe lots and lots of things in new ways, until you have created a pattern of linguistic behavior which will tempt the rising generation to adopt it."[35] Rorty claims that "interesting philosophy is rarely an examination of the pros and cons of a thesis"; rather, "usually it is, explicitly or implicitly, a contest between an entrenched vocabulary which has become a nuisance and a half-formed new vocabulary which vaguely promises great things."[36] Rorty does not wish to engage in "arguments" for or against a given position: in his view, such arguments are bound to be circular or question-begging. Arguments against a "time-honored" vocabulary "are expected to show that central elements in that vocabulary are 'inconsistent in their own terms' or that they 'deconstruct themselves'. But that can *never* be shown."[37] In keeping with his position, Rorty therefore asserts that he is "not going to offer arguments against the vocabulary [he] wants to replace."[38] His purpose, rather, is to encourage his readers to "try to ignore the apparently futile traditional questions" of philosophy by "substituting ... new and possibly interesting questions."[39]

Rorty further claims that there is no reality if, by "reality," we mean something that has its own "intrinsic nature," independent of our symbolizing practices.

---

[34] Richard Rorty, *Contingency, Irony, and Solidarity* (Cambridge: Cambridge University Press, 1989), 9.

[35] Ibid.

[36] Ibid.

[37] Ibid., 8.

[38] Ibid., 9.

[39] Ibid.

Consequently, "truth" is no longer understood as a matter of properly expressing the way things are, because this would suggest that there is something already there to which our linguistic utterances must be faithful. Language does not *express* the truth, but *creates* it. The truth, then, according to Rorty, "is a property of linguistic entities, of sentences"; and hence, the truth "cannot be out there--cannot exist independently of the human mind-- because sentences cannot so exist, or be out there."[40] "Only descriptions of the world can be true or false."[41] As Rorty admits, this is not to say that "the world" is not out there. Rather, it is to say that since only descriptions of the world can be true or false, the "world," whatever that may mean, "on its own ... cannot."[42]

These remarks raise a number of significant questions. If the world, human consciousness, and the divine ground of being do not have an intrinsic nature, then what would it mean to say that they *are*? What kind of reality is it that *is*, and yet has no nature? Rorty might reply that we have not paid enough attention to the irony of the view he espouses. He might point out that since the assertion "these things are, but have no nature" is itself a statement, and since truth is a property of statements and not of reality, he therefore is not attempting to say something true about reality for the simple reason that there is no such truth. One cannot say that reality is truly this or that, because statements of this sort are simply a matter of conventional linguistic description. Even if all this is granted, however, it would appear that, by Rorty's own lights, the world is not as "out there" as he originally suggested. If the nature of reality is determined by linguistic practices, the very notion of a reality independent of those practices becomes senseless. A further question may be asked: How can it be asserted that "the world is *not* out there" if the proposition's contrary has no sense? That is, how

---

[40]Ibid., 5-7.

[41]Ibid., 5.

[42]Ibid.

could this statement be meaningfully affirmed given that negation, as much as affirmation, is contingent on the meaningfulness of the statement in which it occurs?

In response to these questions, Rorty will insist that he is not *arguing* that the notion of "intrinsic nature" is *senseless* or that "there is no truth out there." Rorty rejects such arguments on principle, because they leave any analysis open to the charge of "self-referential inconsistency"--a charge which, in light of his remarks concerning Nietzsche and Derrida, he clearly wishes to avoid.[43] Rorty's position, then, is not based on an argument; it is rather the "recommendation that we in fact *say* little about these topics, and see how we get on."[44]

Rorty's analysis leads him into the awkward position of both affirming and denying the truth of a statement. This being so, we might be tempted, with Aristotle, to refuse to continue a discussion in which our partner insists on transgressing the principle of non-contradiction. A response of this sort would be premature, for we have not yet arrived at the basis of Rorty's apparent misuse of language.

Where, then, does the difficulty lie? When one is playing the traditional philosophic game, statements that deny that reality has an intrinsic nature, for example, are, according to Rorty, correctly understood to be self-refuting; however, when one is not playing the traditional game, when one is playing Rorty's game, such statements are at worst simply "uninteresting." But what does it mean to play Rorty's game? What is it that justifies both the attribution and negation of the charge of self-refutation with regard to the same statement? The short answer, is nothing at all. Nothing can justify

---

[43]Rorty writes: "Nietzsche has caused a lot of confusion by inferring from 'truth is not a matter of correspondence to reality' to 'what we call "truths" are just useful lies.' The same confusion is occasionally found in Derrida, in the inference from 'there is no such reality as the metaphysicians have hoped to find' to 'what we call "real" is not really real.' Such confusions make Nietzsche and Derrida liable to charges of self-referential inconsistency--to claiming to know what they themselves claim cannot be known" (Ibid., 8).

[44]Ibid.

Rorty's position while we are still playing the traditional game, precisely because there are no commensurating criteria for evaluation. As Rorty asserts, "if the new language is really new, there will be no such criteria."[45] This applies as much to the question of meaning, as to the question of justification. One cannot find a commensurate meaning, because to do so would be to speak the old language. "An attempt to state that meaning [the new meaning] would be an attempt to find some familiar (that is, literal) use of words--some sentence which already had a place in the language game--and, to claim that one might just as well have *that*."[46] Hence, in terms of the old language (i.e., the traditional one), the new remark, utterance, gesture, or proposition *has no meaning*.

It would appear that the moment we try to engage Rorty in a critical discussion of the content of his position, we are informed that, in terms of our perspective, the position has no content or meaning. This response is somewhat puzzling, for Rorty appears to be using the same words as we are, he seems to be speaking *our language*. Rorty's reply to this dilemma would likely be as follows: "I am, indeed, using the same words; however, in the context of my vocabulary--my language game--these words have undergone a *change of meaning*." However, Rorty's "change of meaning" is suspect. This new meaning has not yet revealed itself as having any meaning at all. Therefore, we cannot determine whether it is a legitimate one; we cannot even assess whether it is, in fact, a "new meaning."

Rorty defends what Voegelin has described as "the Humpty-Dumpty philosophy of language," a philosophy of language in which "determining the meanings of words is an exercise of the intellectual's power that must not be submitted to criticism" (*AR*, 97). Once in place, a misunderstanding of this sort has far-reaching consequences. For example, Rorty claims that philosophy is simply a matter of "redescribing" or "explaining" things in new and interesting ways. In reality, this view explains nothing

---

[45]Ibid., 9.

[46]Ibid., 18.

at all. When reality is conceived as a manifestation of the unguided symbolic movements of consciousness, there is nothing left for language to explain.

Our argument may be summarized as follows: Rorty claims that sameness and difference, thisness and thatness, are not intrinsic to reality, but are the product of our symbolizing practices. Both the truth and meaning of a given description must admit of linguistic articulation in order to be intelligible. Rorty also claims that his vocabulary is new, that it is a different form of symbolization. However, when we ask him to make clear what this difference is, we are told that it cannot be articulated because the vocabulary is new and there are therefore no commensurating criteria whereby a comparison would be possible. Rorty contradicts himself. In order to articulate his position, he must transgress the position's central thesis, namely, the idea that if there is to be a "difference," it must be manifested in language. To this point in our analysis, we have not been able to determine whether Rorty's position is legitimate, because we have not been able to determine whether it is, in fact, a position. Each time we question him concerning the content of what he says, we are informed that our question cannot be asked because it derives its meaning from a "traditional" philosophic game--a game that Rorty is not playing.

Like Marx, Rorty prohibits the Question. He does so, however, not by claiming to have achieved a comprehensive understanding of reality, but by denying that there is any reality to be comprehended. While Marx, from his "divine" perspective, claims to have comprehended the divine mystery of reality as it becomes luminous in history, Rorty, from his equally divine vantage point, claims to have discovered that there is no such mystery and, hence, nothing to be comprehended.

CONCLUSION

Throughout the course of this work, we have attempted to articulate Voegelin's understanding of a true theology. As we indicated in the Introduction, such an analysis, in order to account for the full range of phenomena covered by the term, necessarily had to include a discussion of the nature of consciousness and the manner in which that consciousness manifests itself symbolically. The reason for this is that the term *theologia*, according to its author, denotes not merely the nature of one's speech concerning the divine, but the character of the soul expressed in speech. Hence, we were faced with the task of a philosophical analysis of consciousness, an analysis of the structures of consciousness and their manifestation in the historical field of symbols. This was our justification for examining what are nominally "religious" questions concerning transcendence in the context of Voegelin's philosophy of consciousness.

The outlining of a true theology did not mark the end of our endeavours. Plato, when he coined the term *theologia*, did so in the context of a discussion of both positive and negative responses to divine reality. The term *theologia* originally occurred in the phrase *typoi peri theologias* (types of theology), which was intended to be descriptive of all the ways in which one can respond to divine reality, ranging from the loving quest for God, to indifference, to the radical denial of God's existence. The analysis of consciousness in a state of order, therefore, had to be carried out alongside an analysis of disordered states of consciousness. The need for this wider theological discussion is not merely a matter of interpretive fidelity--not simply a matter of being true to Plato or Voegelin. Textual fidelity might have a hermeneutical justification, but not necessarily a philosophical one. Rather, proper justification derives from the fact that the symbolic form--the linguistic manifestation--reflects a genuine form of insight into the nature of human existence, something which holds universally. This is precisely what we have attempted to articulate throughout this work. We have attempted to indicate how Voegelin's philosophy of consciousness, when worked out in the context of Plato's understanding of theology, makes possible a coherent and comprehensive analysis of the nature of human existence and the character of its responsive movements toward divine reality.

Some questions remain, however--questions that must be addressed if our conception of a true theology is to be made compelling: (1) How does one move from a state of disorder to a true state of existence--a state constituted by a proper response to the divine? (2) How is this true state to be established as true? As we indicated in the Introduction, the former question pertains to the matter of *paideia* (education) and *periagoge* (turning around), while the latter pertains to the problem of proof.

1. *Paideia* and *Periagoge*

In his analysis of Plato's *Republic*, Voegelin identifies the notions of ascent and descent as integral to the meaning of the work as a whole. He indicates that Plato actually "speaks of the *epanodos*, the ascent of the soul from the day that is night (*nykterine*) to the true (*alethine*) day...almost technically as a definition of 'true philosophy'" (*OH* III, 59). Philosophy is the erotic movement of the human spirit toward wisdom and truth, the movement from the darkness of existence in the Cave to existence in the light of the divine ground. However, the ascent, the movement upward, is balanced by the movement of descent. Socrates, in the Prologue to the dialogue, makes his way down to the Piraeus with Glaukon. "I went down (*kateben*) to the Piraeus yesterday with Glaukon, the son of Ariston" (*Rep*, 327a) It is with this act of descent, this movement down from Athens to the harbor, that the dialogue's erotic ascent begins. It would seem that the truth discovered through the act of ascent is in some way connected to, or contingent upon, an act of descent.

As Voegelin argues, this relation between the movements of ascent and descent is not merely a curious literary feature of the dialogue's Prologue. Rather, it is a theme that occurs throughout the *Republic* as a matrix for the analysis. More specifically, beyond the remarks of the Prologue, it manifests itself in both the Parable of the Cave and the Pamphylian myth at the close of Book X. In the former, the philosopher, once freed from the chains that hold him captive in the cave, makes his way up toward the light of the *Agathon* (the good). However, the fact of this upward movement presupposes that the philosopher is indeed *in the cave*. The notion of ascent makes sense only in relation to the notion of existence in the depth. It is somehow in the depth, in the darkness of the subterranean existence of the Cave, that the ascent begins.

If we turn to the Pamphylian myth, we discover similar parallels. Er, the Pamphylian, descends into Hades and then returns with the story that "will save us if we believe it" (621b). In terms of its content, the myth describes how the dead souls, after having spent a thousand years either below the earth in a state of suffering and anguish or in heaven where they have gazed upon "incredibly beautiful sights," are ushered before the seat of Lachesis in order to establish the next stage of their sojourn. At this point they are instructed:

> This is the message of Lachesis, the maiden of Necessity. Souls of the day, this is the beginning of another mortal round that will bring death. Your guardian spirit will not be assigned to you, you will choose him. Let him who has the first lot be the first to choose a life which will of necessity be his. Virtue knows no master, each will possess it in greater or lesser degree according as he honours or disdains it. The responsibility is his who makes the choice, the god has none (Ibid., 617d-e).

The message makes clear the nature of the decision. Man, with his existence as the stake, must choose his destiny. However, man's ability to choose well depends on the degree to which he has neglected or cultivated his soul, the degree to which he has formed his existence through the pursuit of wisdom or deformed it through thoughtless acquiescence to the standards of his day. One cannot choose more wisely than one in fact is. It is at this point that the myth's descriptive powers come into full view, for here is described the situation of all men at the point of decision between their past and their future. And, as Voegelin asserts, "on that occasion is revealed the value of certain types of life" (*OH* III, 56).

Many in the modern world have attempted to describe this moment of decision, this moment of freedom. In most instances, however, the event is almost completely emptied of significance. For example, Rorty, although recognizing that human existence, due to its contingency, is characterized by an unending series of such moments, undermines the gravity of the situation through an egalitarian levelling of the possible consequences of one's choice. Nothing is lost through a bad decision, because there is nothing there to lose. At its best, such a choice is merely the playful selecting of a new self, in similar fashion to the way one selects one's trousers for the day. At its worst, it is little more than the boring task of continually deciding what one will be. Happily, Rorty's position is not exhaustive with regard to contemporary discussions of the problem. For example, Albert Camus, in his novel *The Fall*, articulates with stark clarity the weight of freedom at the moment of decision. Following an admission of his former passion for freedom, as well as his misplaced veneration of it, the character Jean-Baptiste describes the matter negatively:

> I didn't know that freedom is not a reward or a decoration that is celebrated with champagne. Nor yet a gift, a box of dainties designed to make you lick your chops. Oh, no! It's a chore, on the contrary, and a long-distance race, quite solitary and very exhausting. No champagne, no friends raising their glasses as they look at you affectionately. Alone in a forbidding room, alone to decide in face of oneself or in the face of others' judgment. At the end of all freedom is a court sentence; that's why freedom is too heavy to bear, especially when you're down with a fever, or are distressed, or love nobody.[47]

This passage, for all its deficiencies, is a shining light when placed alongside the understanding of freedom given in modern liberalism. It reveals a deep recognition of

---

[47]Albert Camus, *The Fall*, J. O'Brien, trans. (New York: Random House, 1956), 132-33.

the gravity of the situation at the point at which a decision is required, a gravity that a liberal ironist like Rorty does not understand.

However, Camus, although realizing the implications of the event, appears hard-pressed to find hope at the moment of decision. The freedom experienced at the dead point of decision is a "court sentence," something "too heavy to bear," and this because no help is to be found. One is "alone in a forbidding room," solitary, and "without one's friends." The best Camus seems able to manage is the proviso that the despairing nature of the situation might be lessened if one were at least to love somebody, if there was another toward whom one's spirit were to move lovingly. What Camus here understands to be merely a mitigating factor regarding a desperate situation is for both Voegelin and Plato the existential ground whereby the experience of hope is made possible.

Love, if it does not turn in on itself, is a movement of the spirit toward that which is "other." In this sense, the possiblity of its manifestation is dependent on the fact that another does indeed exist. However, love is equally something that is native to the spirit of the lover, an event only possible if there is a lover who can love. Both lover and beloved are necessary in order for the event to occur. It is at this point that Plato's dialectic of ascent and descent becomes significant.

In our discussion of the *Republic's* Prologue, its Parable of the Cave and its Pamphylian myth, we saw that the truth of reality can be discovered through the action of ascent and descent. As Voegelin states, "the truth brought up from the Piraeus by Socrates in his discourse, and the truth brought up from Hades by the messenger Er, are the same truth that is brought down by the philosopher who has seen the Agathon" (*OH* III, 60). However, the fact that truth can be found both in the depth of Hades and the region beyond the Cave, is, Voegelin writes, a rather "disquieting" thought. It is reminiscent of the Heraclitian paradox: "The way up and the way down is one and the same" (Ibid.). The fact that the *same* truth can be found in both domains does not imply that there is no difference between them. Life in the darkness of the Cave, in Hades, or in the egalitarian *politeia* (form of government) of the Piraeus, remains a deficient form of existence. Plato's insight, rather, is that even in such states of darkness, the structure of human existence in tension toward the divine remains constant. Although human beings are free to disregard the structure of their own existence, free to deny the reality of the divine ground as an ordering force in consciousness, they cannot abolish it. As Voegelin asserts,

> there is no other reality than that of which we have experience. When a person refuses to live in existential tension toward the ground, it is not the 'world' that is thereby changed but rather he who loses contact with reality and in his own person suffers a loss of reality. Since that does not make him cease to be a man, and since his consciousness continues to function within the form of reality, he will generate *ersatz* images of reality in order to obtain order and direction for his existence and action in the world (*Anamnesis*, 170).

The constancy of the structure of reality grounds the claim that truth can be found both through a descent into the Cave and an ascent to the region beyond it. Truth must be present even in the darkness of the Cave, for were it not, the very possibility of ascent would be undermined. There do not exist two worlds between which one must attempt to move by some purely human act of cognition. Rather, there is one reality, a reality that, depending on the nature of one's response, is more or less adequately understood, articulated, and lived in. One can certainly live in darkness, yet the darkness too is circumscribed by the structure of the Cosmos.

The constancy of reality is precisely the basis for the hope we found lacking in Camus's analysis. Even if one dwells in the Cave, even if one has deformed one's true humanity, one is still a human being. And given that human existence is constituted by its relation to transcendence, even in the darkest of places the light of the divine can manifest itself in consciousness. It is this light which constitutes the basis of hope. For although hope is in that which is unseen; although it is not directed to a thing that exists in space and time; although the dimension of reality toward which it is directed can be found both through ascent and descent, it is not a hope *against* reality. Voegelin writes: "The apparently hopeless situation of the soul at the point of its death--that it has the freedom of Arete (virtue) but not the wisdom to use it--is not hopeless; forces of life are there to help. But the source of the help is hidden; we can only say that it is There" (*OH* III, 62). The loving, responsive movement of human beings toward the divine reality that, in terms of human cognition, always remains "hidden" gives direction at the apparently hopeless moment of decision.

In light of this analysis of consciousness in its movements of ascent and descent, the nature and intent of education can now be clarified. Fundamentally, we must say that education (*paideia*) is not a matter of forming consciousness into something it is not already. It is not a matter of putting "information" or "knowledge" (*episteme*) into souls that hitherto did not possess it. Rather, it is an attempt to lead man, with his concrete consciousness, to a truer understanding of his own nature, a nature that, however deformed or covered over, precedes the pedagogical event. This conception of education therefore rests on the idea that human consciousness is characterized by a structure that obtains universally, one that holds even when the light of truth has dimmed in the Cave. The truth and reality of human existence in tension toward the divine must be there, for without it the educative ascent would not be an *ascent* at all, but simply movement.

The way in which this educative process is carried out in the concrete varies considerably. One may begin, like Voegelin, with a critical analysis of corrupt symbols in an attempt to provoke understanding; one may engage a partner in dialogue in order to lead him to a truth already present, albeit inarticulately, in consciousness; or one might, as does Plato, write dramas or plays that point up the truth of human existence. Regardless of the method, fundamental to the pedagogical endeavor is what Plato has called the *periagoge*, the "turning around" of the soul. In accordance with what we have argued throughout this work, a false (*pseudos*) theology is not simply the result of an analytic error, i.e., a mistake in logic. Sophists, both ancient and modern, have for centuries advanced logically consistent arguments that result in the ridiculous conclusion that there is no reality. The difficulty here is that logic's purely formal structure makes it susceptible to the cause of infidelity. One can argue in a perfectly consistent manner on the formal level while at the same time saying unequivocally false things about the nature of existence. Logic is a purely secondary phenomenon. The real difficulty is one pertaining to the state of one's soul; therefore, if any restorative measures are to be employed to resolve the matter, they must begin at precisely this point. Those who speak improperly about the gods do so, not because they are not clever enough or, as Voegelin states, because they are "wanting in intellectual acumen" (*QDD*, 576). Rather, they do so because experientially they have lost touch with divine reality. The possibility of a return to this truth is therefore dependent on a regaining of the experience of the transcendent. According to Plato, this is possible only if one turns one's gaze from the shadowy images on the wall of the Cave to the light that shines from beyond. As Voegelin asserts, following Plato, from this state one can return to the truth of reality only through a "turning around (*periagoge*) of the whole soul from ignorance to the truth of God, from opinion about uncertainly wavering things to knowledge of being, and from multifarious activity to the justice of tending to one's proper sphere of action" (*OH* III, 68). Conversely, if one insists on gazing upon the shadowy images on the wall of the Cave--if one refuses to turn around--the divine light will be obscured and the movement of ascent will become significantly more difficult. However, this need not be the case. The notion of *periagoge* indicates that the possibility of gaining a truer understanding of reality is not dependent on the addition of something not already present in consciousness. True knowledge (*episteme*) cannot be put into a soul "that does not possess it" in the same manner that one cannot insert "vision into blind eyes" (*Rep.*, 518c). The faculty by which man sees the "brightest region of being," the *Agathon* (the good), is something already present in consciousness (Ibid., 518c-d). Hence, education (*paideia*) is the art of turning (*periagoge*) one's "organ of vision" toward the divine light, of directing it toward what is True, Good, and Beautiful.

2. Proof, Logic, and Existence

The second question to be discussed pertains to the matter of proof, to the question of how the insights implicit in a true theology--those gained through an act of "turning around"--are determined to be so. We must first determine for what one is being asked when one is asked for a proof. More specifically, we must clarify the different meanings of the term "proof," its various forms, and the dimensions of reality to which these forms pertain. By thus clarifying the matter, we will be able to point up the wrong-headedness of a number of common assumptions regarding the nature of proof, assumptions under which theologians and philosophers have laboured endlessly in their attempt to prove the existence of God. To hint at our conclusion, the truth of a given form of speech concerning the gods, i.e., a given *theologia*, is not primarily a matter of demonstration but of seeing aright, a form of vision or understanding that is not so much a question of logic as it is of character.

The various dimensions of reality taken together form a unified whole, a cosmos. The adjective "unified" does not denote, as has been so often claimed by the positivists and empiricists of the twentieth century, a relation of sameness, but rather the ordered coexistence and interpenetration of significantly different realms of being. In Voegelin's terms, the Cosmos is a "primordial community of being." If reality is constituted by different levels of being, then it follows that there are corresponding modes of cognition and, in turn, forms of proof that correspond to these various modes. The acceptable or appropriate type of proof to be used in a given situation is to be determined by the dimension of reality in question. If this principle is violated, if one stipulates in advance the type of proof to be employed without due consideration for what it is one is attempting to prove, more often than not the result will be misunderstanding. For example, if one claims that the only legitimate form of proof is empirical verification-- empirical verification in the sense called for by thinkers like A. J. Ayer--then quite obviously a great deal of reality will have to go, the most notable part of which is the divine ground.

However, no intelligent believer has ever claimed that the existence of God can be modelled on the existence of objects and events in the spatio-temporal world. As Voegelin writes, "back of the desire to prove the existence of God is a transfer of the term existence from the model of an object in time and space to a reality which is not an object in time and space (which nobody would insist on anyway)" (*Conversations*, 53). No such proof is required; there is nothing of the sort to prove, because God, the divine ground, "is a sort of non-existent reality, a *reality* but not in the mode of being or existence of an object in the spatio-temporal world" (*Conversations*, 51). Voegelin continues:

> If you don't insist in the first place that he [God] is an existent like other objects in time and space, then you don't have to prove his existence because you never said he existed. You have him in consciousness already present, already there, and you do not have to transfer the concept of existence of an object in time and space to God and afterwards prove his existence (Ibid., 52).

Voegelin's argument is simple: you must prove the existence of God if and only if God exists. God, however, does not exist. Therefore, God's existence does not need to be proven.

Although the argument is logically consistent, the second premise will certainly invite question. To the sceptic, Voegelin's argument will likely appear to be merely a linguistic sleight of hand used to circumvent a genuine critical discussion, or a dubious semantic game played with the terms "existence" and "reality." To others, it might seem that the argument, although effective in handling the sceptic's demand for proof, does so at too high a price, i.e., it does so only to invite a host of far more pernicious philosophical challenges. Both of these responses, however, miss the point of Voegelin's analysis. When Voegelin says that God is a non-existent reality, there is no semantic game being played. The assertion that God does not exist is delivered with absolute seriousness. Voegelin is attempting to rid us of the deeply entrenched penchant to speak about all reality as if it were a thing. God is not an existing thing whose presence eludes us because we are separated by a large chasm of space and time. He is not a being we could glimpse if we only had a more powerful telescope; he is not a "thing," the existence of which could be established through deductive or inductive demonstration. To think in this way is to invite the altogether foolish metaphysical debates about God's substance and place in the Cosmos, criticized in the familiar antinomies of Kant's *Critique of Pure Reason.* The problem is not one of proof, but of the removal of methodological restrictions that inhibit understanding and prevent us from seeing something that is already present in consciousness.

In light of these remarks, the question arises as to why thinkers such as Plato and Anselm, thinkers whom Voegelin commends for having understood the nature of the problem, both apparently offer proofs for God's existence. In the case of Anselm, Voegelin makes it clear that the *Proslogion* is not an attempt to prove the existence of God, but a "prayer" in response to the movement of the Spirit. As Voegelin points out, the term "proof" does not even occur in the *Proslogion*, "but only in the discussion with Gaunilo" (*Conversations*, 52). "There is no reason why the term should be used in the *Proslogion*; for when the believer explores the rational structure of his faith the existence of God is not in question" (Ibid.).

If this is so, then why does the term occur at all? According to Voegelin, Anselm, in his response to Gaunilo, "must use the term 'proof' because Gaunilo acts the role of the fool, of the insipiens, who says 'there is no God' and assumes that the explorer of faith is engaged in a 'proof' for the assertion that God exists" (Ibid.). It would seem that the positive propositions concerning God's existence are a manifestation, not of the believer's quest for the divine, but of the confrontation between the believer and the one who claims "there is no God." Once the fool enters the discussion, "the noetic quest threatens to derail into a quarrel about proof or non-proof of a proposition" (*QDD*, 576).

The term "fool" is the English translation of the Latin *insipiens* and the Hebrew *nabal.* As Voegelin indicates, the English translation is perhaps not the best. The term derives from the Latin *follis*, which means "bellows or wind-bag," notions which carry with them a sense of "silliness or lack of judgment." However, the Hebrew *nabal*, the fool of Psalm 13, "is certainly not a man wanting in intellectual acumen or worldly judgment" (Ibid.). Rather, the term is descriptive of those "who do evil rather than good because they do not 'seek after God' and his justice" (Ibid., 577). It indicates a contemptuous response to the divine which manifests itself "in ruthless conduct toward the weaker man and [creates] general disorder in society" (Ibid.). The fool of the psalm is one who brings about disorder, both in society and his personal existence, through a negative response to the divine appeal. However, his "contemptuous folly," although capable of rising to the radical denial of God's existence, does not seem to do so. "The fool stands against the revealed God, he does not stand against a *fides quaerens intellectum*" (*QQD*, 577). In the debate between Anselm and Gaunilo, this *fides* is precisely what is at issue. The existential foolishness of the *nabal* has become a radical challenge to the noetic quest itself, a challenge that was first clarified analytically in the work of Plato.

In the *Republic* and the *Laws*, Plato addresses the matter of the radical denial of divine reality through an examination of the following triadic propositional set. According to Voegelin, the propositions are likely a Sophistic school product in that they share the same structure as a set of propositions found in Gorgias's essay "On Being":

(1)   It seems that no gods exist;
(2)   Even if they do exist, they do not care about men;
(3)   Even if they care about men they can be propitiated by gifts.

For Voegelin, as for Plato, the negative propositions rest on a denial of divine reality as an ordering force in man's experience. In order for such an argument "to be plausible in the fourth century B.C., the denial had to be couched in the form of a counter-myth of the Hesiodian type" (*QDD*, 579). The particular form assumed by the counter-myth responding to the negative propositions was that of a cosmogony in which "the gods of the myth are replaced by the elements in the material sense as the 'oldest' creative reality" (Ibid., 578). Plato argues that reality could not have originated in the movements of purely material forces or elements. Voegelin summarizes Plato's argument as follows:

> There is no self-moving matter; the patterned network of cause and effect must be caused in its turn by a movement that originates outside the network; and the only reality we know to be self-moving is the Psyche. Hence, in a genetic construction of Being, the elements cannot function as the 'oldest' reality; only the divine Psyche, as experienced by the human psyche, can be 'oldest' in the sense of the self-movement in which all ordered movement in the world originates (Ibid., 578).

The positive propositions that Plato then derives from this argument are as follows:

(1)   The gods exist;
(2)   They do care about man;
(3)   And they cannot be made accomplices in human criminality by offering them bribes from the profits of crime.

As Voegelin asserts, Plato's positive argument "is not a 'proof' in the sense of a logical demonstration, of an *apodeixis*," and this in the same way that the negative argument is not a 'dis-proof' (*QQD*, 578). Rather, it is a proof in the sense of an *epideixis*, "a pointing to an area of reality which the constructor of the negative propositions has chosen to overlook, or to ignore, or to refuse to perceive" (Ibid., 579).

Voegelin's distinction between apodictic and epidictic proofs will certainly not be well received by those with a penchant for logical demonstration. It will be viewed as a dubious attempt to avoid the rigour of logical analysis, to sidestep a genuine critical discussion. Such objections fail to see that logic has nothing to do with the testing of the legitimacy of our basic existential commitments. In this realm of discourse, logic is a purely secondary phenomenon.

On the most general level, we must assert with Voegelin that "one cannot prove reality by a syllogism" (Ibid.). Reality is either there or it is not; it is something one sees or does not see. Nothing more, in terms of proof, can be had. The reason for this is quite simple: if one were to attempt to prove reality, one would have to do so in terms of something else. However, if one appeals to "something else," the question then arises as to what this something is, whether it, too, is a dimension of reality, or something other than reality. Quite obviously, it cannot be something other than reality, for if this were the case, then one would be in the precarious position of proving the existence of something real through an appeal to something that is not. However, if the "something else" is real, then the initial question concerning the first reality will necessarily have to be extended to the second on which the logical demonstration rests, raising the spectre of an infinite regress of proofs that cannot, by definition, ever reach a satisfactory conclusion.

The impossibility of a deductive proof for the structures of reality does not imply a deficiency. The fact that Plato's argument can do no more than point to various dimensions of reality that have been overlooked does not mean that it is an inferior form of proof. To concede this point would be to accept the logician's claim that formal demonstration is the only acceptable type of proof, with the proviso that man is in the lamentable position of not being able to employ such a method with regard to the most pressing questions of his existence.

This was the position of many of the existentialist thinkers of the late nineteenth and early twentieth centuries. Even Camus, although seeing clearly enough the inadequacies of modern analytic thinking, accepted such thinking as the paradigm of rational inquiry. At the end of his work *The Myth of Sisyphus*, Camus comes to the sad conclusion that human existence is absurd. The predicate "absurd," like the predicate "irrational," has sense only in relation to a standard of meaningfulness and rationality. This standard is evident throughout Camus's writings, even though Camus has difficulty in expressing it. It is only by its measure that Camus's affirmation of absurdity can be understood. In other words, his statement that existence is absurd belies a deep acceptance of the conception of reason it finds wanting. The difficulty is that Camus, although realizing the inadequacy of that conception of reason, could not find an alternative to it, could not see his way clear to reject the hegemony of logical analysis in order to positively articulate other forms of knowing and proof.[48]

For both Plato and Voegelin, proof is not a matter of demonstration, but of pointing. Through myth, argument, and the concrete order of one's existence, one points to an area of reality that the doubter has failed to recognize. The doubter's failure to perceive, however, is not merely an "analytical error." His lack of vision is not simply

---

[48]It should be noted that this dilemma is characteristic of Camus's early work. In his later work he attempts to move beyond the notion of absurdity in order to articulate a fuller understanding of human existence. See Albert Camus, *The Plague*, S. Gilbert, trans. (London: Penguin Books, 1960) and Albert Camus, *The Rebel*, A. Bower, trans. (New York: Vintage Books, Inc., 1956).

a matter of language. Rather, as we have argued throughout this work, language does not stand on its own, but is a manifestation of the state of one's soul. Therefore, in the case of the soul that articulates itself symbolically by means of the negative propositions, what is revealed is the existence of one who has lost contact with the divine as an ordering force in existence. As Voegelin asserts, following Plato, "the 'ignorance within the soul' (*en te psyche agnoia*) is 'truly the falsehood' (*alethos pseudos*), while the falsehood in words is only an after-rising image (*hysteron gegonon eidolon*)" (*QDD*, 579).

One's apprehension of the truth of reality is not simply a matter of intellectual prowess or clever reasoning, but of the degree to which one has formed one's existence in openness toward reality. One's ability to see aright is dependent on the state of one's soul. And souls can be formed either through a willingness to perceive or through an existential closure that prohibits one from seeing the reality of both the Cosmos in which one dwells and the nature of one's own existence. The nature of this refusal to apperceive, as we have seen in the work of Marx, may be so pathological as to cause one to deny the reality of one's own existence, even when that reality is unavoidably present to consciousness.

In coining the term *theologia*, Plato understood that the radical denial of divine reality is as much a type of theology as the loving quest for it. Both are responses to the divine. As Voegelin asserts, "both types, the negative as well as the positive, are theologies, because both express a human response to the divine appeal; they both are, in Plato's language, the verbal mimesis respectively of man's existence in truth or falsehood" (Ibid., 580).

Given our distinction between forms of theological speech and the states of existence they express, it follows that Plato's positive propositions, in the same way as the negative Sophistic triad, have no autonomous truth; they do not stand on their own, but rather are true only insofar as they manifest consciousness' movement toward the divine. In Voegelin's language, "they would be just as empty as the negative ones, if they were not backed by the reality of the divine-human movement and countermovement, of the Prayer answering the appeal in the soul of the proponent" (Ibid.). If the positive propositions of Plato's proof are not understood in this way, they too can become dogma. They too can become empty when they cease to recall to the mind of the listener the engendering experiences to which they first gave expression. However, if the symbols are understood aright, they continue to point to the truth of human existence in tension toward the divine.

Language is a means through which consciousness manifests itself; it is a medium through which the structure of human existence can be analytically clarified; but it is also a medium through which consciousness can hide or distort that structure. Nevertheless, the structures of human existence cannot be abolished. Amidst the changing movements of consciousness in history, the changing symbolic forms, and the concrete political structures in which they manifest themselves, something remains the same. As Voegelin states, "what is constant in the history of mankind, i.e., in the time dimension of existence, is the structure of existence itself" (*EESH*, 220). Concerning the content of this constant, Voegelin's concluding remarks from the final volume of *Order and History* are appropriate:

> The super-constant above the constants is not a principle of order whose proper application will dissolve the disorder of Cosmic order, but the experience of the paradoxic tension in formative reality, of the tension between the divine reality experienced as formatively present at the ordering pole of the tensions and the divine reality experienced as a Beyond of its concrete manifestations in the process, between the God who reveals himself in his presence in time and the God who remains the experienced but unknown reality beyond time. Moreover, the paradoxic tension in the revelation of formative reality is experienced as ultimate in the sense that intelligibly it cannot be out-experienced or out-symbolized by further experiences of reality. This experienced ultimacy of the tension becomes luminous in the symbol 'divine' (*OH* V, 106-7).

BIBLIOGRAPHY

Works by Eric Voegelin

Anamnesis. Gerhart Niemeyer, trans. & ed. Notre Dame: University of Notre Dame Press, 1978.

Autobiographical Reflections. E. Sandoz, ed. Baton Rouge: Louisiana State University Press, 1989.

Conversations with Eric Voegelin. E. O'Connor, ed. Montreal: Thomas More Institute, 1980.

"Equivalences of Experience and Symbolization in History," *Philosophical Studies*, XXVIII, 88-103, 1981.

From Enlightenment to Revolution. J. H. Hallowell, ed. Durham: Duke University Press, 1975.

"Immortality: Experience and Symbol," *Harvard Theological Review*, 60: 3, 235-279, 1967.

"Industrial Society in Search of Reason," *World Technology and Human Destiny*, R. Aron, ed. Michigan: University of Michigan Press, 1963.

"Response to Professor Altizer's 'A New History and a New but Ancient God'," *Journal of the American Academy of Religion*, XLIII, 765-772, 1975.

Israel and Revelation, Baton Rouge: Louisiana State University Press. Vol. I of *Order and History*, 1956.

The World of the Polis, Baton Rouge: Louisiana State University Press. Vol. II of *Order and History*, 1957.

Plato and Aristotle, Baton Rouge: Louisiana State University Press. Vol. III of *Order and History*, 1957.

The Ecumenic Age, Baton Rouge: Louisiana State University Press. Vol. IV of *Order and History*, 1974.

In Search of Order, Baton Rouge: Louisiana State University Press. Vol. V of *Order and History*, 1987.

"Quod Deus Dicitur," *Journal of the American Academy of Religion*, 53/3, 569-584, 1985.

Additional Sources

Altizer, Thomas. "A New History and a New but Ancient God," *Journal of the American Academy of Religion*, XLIII, 757-764, 1975.

Bloom, Allan. *The Closing of the American Mind*. New York: Simon and Schuster, 1987.

Camus, Albert. *The Fall*. J. O'Brian, trans. New York: Random House, 1956.

Davidson, Donald. *Inquiries into Truth and Interpretation*. Oxford: Oxford University Press, 1984.

Derrida, Jacques. *Dissemination*. B. Johnson, trans. Chicago: The University of Chicago Press, 1981.

Feuerbach, Ludwig. *The Essence of Christianity*. G. Eliot, trans., New York: Prometheus Books, 1989.

Griswold, Charles. *Self-Knowledge in Plato's Phaedrus*. New Haven: Yale University Press, 1986.

Hegel, G. W. F. *Hegel: The Essential Writings*. F. G. Weiss, trans. & ed. New York: Harper and Row, Publishers, 1974.

James, William. *Essays in Radical Empiricism*. F. Burkhardt & F. Bowers, eds. Massachusetts: Harvard University Press, 1976.

McKnight, Stephen. *Eric Voegelin's Search for Order in History*. Baton Rouge: Louisiana State University Press, 1978.

Rorty, Richard. *Contingency, Irony, and Solidarity*. Cambridge: Cambridge University Press, 1989.

Taylor, Mark. *Erring: A Postmodern A/theology*. Chicago: The University of Chicago Press, 1984.

Plato. *The Collected Dialogues*. E. Hamilton & H. Cairns, eds., New Jersey: Princeton University Press, 1963.

Wittgenstein, Ludwig. *Culture and Value*. P. Winch, trans. Chicago: The University of Chicago Press, 1980.

INDEX